MUHAMMAD ALI

"I Am the Greatest"

Carin T. Ford

Series Consultant:
Dr. Russell L. Adams, Chairman
Department of
Afro-American Studies,
Howard University

Enslow Publishers, Inc.

40 Industrial Road   PO Box 38
Box 398   Aldershot
Berkeley Heights, NJ 07922   Hants GU12 6BP
USA   UK

http://www.enslow.com

"I AM THE GREATEST.
NOT ONLY DO I KNOCK 'EM OUT, I PICK THE ROUND!"
—*Muhammad Ali*

Library of Congress Cataloging-in-Publication Data

Muhammad Ali : "I am the greatest" / Carin T. Ford.
      p. cm.—(African-American biography library)
   Includes bibliographical references and index.
   ISBN 0-7660-2460-1 (hardcover)
   1. Ali, Muhammad, 1942–Juvenile literature. 2. Boxers (Sports)—United States—
Biography—Juvenile literature.   I. Title. II. Series.
GV1132.A4F67 2006
796.83'092-dc22
                                                                2005019748

Printed in the United States of America

10 9 8 7 6 5 4 3 2 1

To Our Readers:
We have done our best to make sure all Internet Addresses in this book were active and appro-
priate when we went to press. However, the author and the publisher have no control over and
assume no liability for the material available on those Internet sites or on other Web sites they
may link to. Any comments or suggestions can be sent by e-mail to comments@enslow.com or
to the address on the back cover.

Every effort has been made to locate all copyright holders of material used in this book. If any
errors or omissions have occurred, corrections will be made in future editions of this book.

Illustration Credits: AP/Wide World, pp. 3, 4, 8, 14, 17, 22, 30, 35, 38, 41, 42, 45, 50, 56, 61,
63, 66, 68, 74, 76, 78, 82, 84, 86, 88, 94, 96, 100, 103, 109, 110, 112, 114, 116; Library of
Congress, pp. 12, 32.

Cover Illustrations: AP/Wide World

Contents

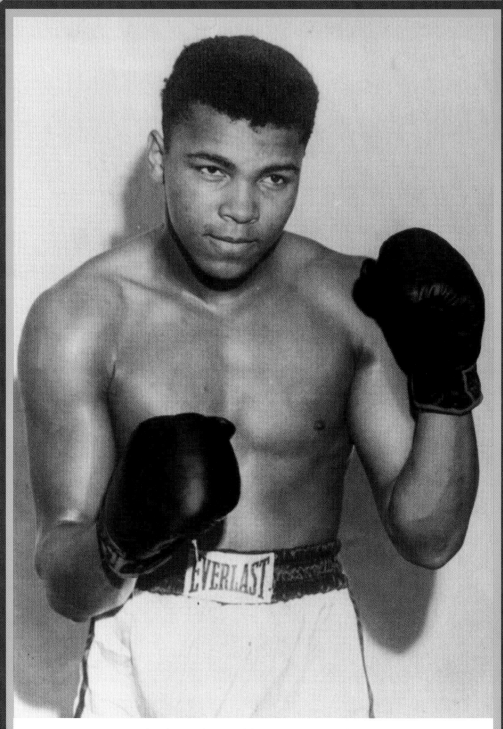

Cassius Clay later changed his name to Muhammad Ali.

❖ ❖ ❖ ❖ ❖

Chapter 1

Learning the Ropes

On Cassius Clay's twelfth birthday, in January 1954, his parents gave him a new bicycle. It was a red-and-white Schwinn, and Cassius was very proud of it. One October afternoon, he rode his bicycle with one of his friends to the Columbia Auditorium. The Louisville (Kentucky) Service Club was holding its yearly bazaar there. African-American merchants set up booths and sold a variety of merchandise. Cassius and his friend spent the day walking around the fair and eating the popcorn, ice cream, hot dogs, and candy that were being given away. When it was time to go home, Cassius looked for his bicycle, but it was not where he had left it. He looked all over but could not find it. Someone had stolen his bike. "I was so mad I was crying," he said.[1]

In tears, Cassius went searching for a policeman. He was told he could find an officer in the basement of the building. There was a boxing gym there called the Columbia Gym. Cassius stormed downstairs, upset and angry, yelling that he planned to beat up the person who had stolen his bike.

In the basement, Cassius found Joe Martin, a member of the Louisville police department. Officer Martin also taught youngsters to box at the Columbia Gym. He patiently listened as Cassius shouted and threatened to hurt the thief. Finally, Martin said, "Well, do you know how to fight?"

Cassius answered, "No, but I'd fight anyway."[2]

Martin then made a suggestion that would change Cassius's life. "Why don't you learn something about fighting before you go making any hasty challenges?" he asked.[3]

Cassius looked around the gym. About ten boys were working out—some were hitting the small speed bags, some were jumping rope, others were sparring, or practicing boxing skills in the ring. Cassius's eyes fell on a boy who was shadowboxing in the ring. He could barely follow the quick punches thrown by the boy.

Cassius almost forgot about his stolen bicycle in the midst of the excitement of the boxing gym. Then Martin asked for a description of the bicycle, and Cassius gave him the information. As Cassius turned to leave, Martin mentioned that the gym was open for boxing every weeknight from six until eight o'clock. He handed Cassius an application to join.

Cassius had never boxed in his life. He stuck the application in the pocket of his pants and went home to tell his father about the stolen bike.

A few days later, Cassius was watching television at home. He found himself looking at a program called *Tomorrow's Champions*. The local boxing show was produced by Officer Joe Martin. As Cassius watched Martin working with one of the boys, he remembered the application that Martin had given him. Where was it? His mother had emptied the pockets when she washed his pants. She quickly found the application.

"I want to be a boxer," Cassius said.[4] At first, his parents were unsure about allowing Cassius to go to the boxing gym. But his father finally decided that learning to box would be better than running around with the boys in the neighborhood.

Cassius showed up at Martin's gym. Although he had never worn boxing gloves before, he leaped excitedly into the ring with an older boxer and began punching wildly. Soon his nose was bleeding and he felt dizzy. Someone eventually pulled him out of the ring.

"You'll be all right," another boxer told him. ". . . Get someone to teach you how to do it."[5]

Martin showed Cassius how to place his feet. He also instructed him in throwing a right cross. Other than that,

After just six weeks of learning to box, twelve-year-old Cassius was ready for his first fight.

Cassius was on his own. He liked it, and although his punches were wild, he kept at it.

"Something was driving me and I kept fighting and I kept training. . . . I kept coming back to the gym," he said.[6]

After about six weeks, he had learned the basics of boxing. He was ready to fight his first match and appear on *Tomorrow's Champions*. Cassius was excited that viewers in Kentucky would see him on television. He trained hard all week. His opponent was Ronnie O'Keefe, a young boy who weighed eighty-nine pounds, just like Cassius. They wore large, fourteen-ounce gloves.

The fight lasted three rounds; each round was one minute long. Boxing is a judged sport. Three or more judges watch a boxing match and award points to each fighter based on how many clean punches he lands. Because he landed more punches than O'Keefe, Cassius won by a split decision. This means that two of the three judges gave Cassius more points than they gave Ronnie O'Keefe.

When the announcement was made, Cassius shouted that one day he would become "the greatest of all time."[7]

Chapter 2

Somebody Special

C assius Marcellus Clay Jr. was born January 17, 1942, in Louisville, Kentucky. His father, Cassius Sr., had been named for a white Kentucky farmer who lived in the 1800s and was an abolitionist—a person in favor of ending slavery. That first Cassius Clay was the editor of an antislavery newspaper and later was a diplomat to Russia. After he inherited forty slaves, Clay became one of the first men in Kentucky to free his slaves. Cassius's great-grandfather, who grew up on Clay's plantation, was listed in the Kentucky census as a free black man.

Odessa Grady Clay, Cassius's mother, had two white grandfathers. One, Abe Grady, was a white Irish immigrant who had married an African-American woman. Odessa Clay's other grandfather was the son of a white man and a slave named Dinah.

SOMEBODY SPECIAL

Cassius's mother worked cleaning people's houses. His father painted billboards and signs for a living. Sometimes his father painted religious murals and landscapes. Two years after Cassius was born, the Clays had another son, Rudolph, who was called Rudy.

Although the family was not wealthy, the Clays were part of the middle class of southern African Americans at that time. There was always plenty to eat and the boys had enough clothing.

Young Cassius was always on the go. He did not like sitting still. He enjoyed running and moving about on his tiptoes. He was a confident, talkative boy who was nicknamed "Gee-Gee" because those were his first words, which he had repeated frequently in his crib.[1]

"Everything he did seemed different as a child," said Odessa. ". . . His mind was like the March wind, blowing every which way. And whenever I thought I could predict what he'd do, he turned around and proved me wrong."[2]

Sometimes Cassius went to work with his father. Cassius Clay Sr. taught his son how to draw letters, mix paint, and put the signs together. Young Cassius often helped out by climbing up and down the ladder to take buckets of paint to his father.

At the end of the day, Cassius Clay Sr. liked to relax by singing and dancing. He enjoyed imitating different celebrities, such as singers Nat "King" Cole and Bing

Cassius grew up in Louisville, the biggest city in Kentucky.

Odessa and Cassius Clay Sr.

Odessa Clay was a quiet woman whose days were filled with cooking, sewing, and cleaning. She did not smoke, curse, or drink, and she attended the Baptist Church every Sunday with her children. She always made sure the boys were clean; they were never allowed to walk out of the house barefoot. When she bought groceries at the local store, she always paid cash and refused to put anything on credit.

Cassius Clay Sr., however, did not follow the example set by his wife. He liked to chase women and drink. He was arrested several times for reckless driving, disorderly conduct, and assault and battery. Occasionally he became violent when he was drinking. Three times Odessa Clay called the police and asked them to protect her from her husband.

Crosby. Young Cassius liked watching his father sing and dance.

Cassius and his brother, Rudy, were very close. The boys liked to wrestle, and Cassius always made sure he was the leader. Although many boys in the neighborhood got together to play tackle football, Cassius usually did not participate. He did not like the roughness. Sometimes he would play touch football. It was difficult for anyone to tag him because he was such a fast runner.

From the time they were young, Cassius and his brother,
Rudy, left, liked to wrestle and box.

Other than shooting marbles (and he was an excellent marbles player), Cassius liked asking Rudy to throw rocks at him. As the rocks flew, Cassius would move quickly—side to side, front, back—and dodge them. Rudy threw many rocks at his brother, but never once did a rock hit Cassius.

> "Everything he did seemed different as a child."[3]

Cassius was not a very good student at Virginia Avenue Grade School. Although he had a lot of energy and confidence, and he seemed bright, Cassius was not interested in the subjects he was taught. What he *was* interested in was drawing attention to himself. He said he realized at a very young age that "nearly everybody likes to watch somebody that acts different."[4]

Cassius decided not to ride the bus to school. He preferred to run alongside it. The children on the bus would watch him, and they would wave and shout. During recess, Cassius sometimes started a fight with another student, knowing the other children in the schoolyard would gather around him. "It made me somebody special," he said. ". . . I always liked to draw crowds."[5]

Chapter 3

In Training

A t the Columbia Gym, Cassius was an extremely hard worker. He trained six days a week. Yet he was not popular with the other boys training to become boxers. "He was always bragging that he was the best fighter in the gym and that someday he was going to be champion," said Joe Martin.[1]

But as he watched Cassius train, Martin knew the boy had the potential to become an excellent boxer. Cassius had unusually quick hands and feet. Even in his early fights, judges were impressed by his reflexes. Also, his eyes took in everything. When Cassius saw that he could make a move, his hands responded instantly. In addition to these qualities, Martin saw that Cassius was able to keep calm when there was trouble. He did not lose his composure and start punching wildly. He was brave; he was cool.

Joe Martin said Cassius was the "hardest worker of any kid I ever taught."

Cassius took his training seriously. He would not smoke or drink, and he paid careful attention to what he ate. For breakfast, he drank a quart of milk with two raw eggs. In the school cafeteria at lunch, he filled two trays with six servings of milk, a pile of sandwiches, and plates of hot food. He did not eat junk food. Cassius believed the food he ate would make him a better boxer. "He used to talk about his body being pure, a temple, even when he was a kid," said Beverly Edwards, a classmate.[2]

Although he was training to be a fighter, Cassius was not a bully. He did not pick on other students, and he refused to play football for his high school when the coach asked him. He had played football "just once, that's all," he said. "They gave me the ball and tackled me. My helmet hit the ground. POW. No, Sir. You got to get hit in that game, tooooo rough. You don't have to get hit in boxing, people don't understand that."[3]

Cassius was fairly shy, and it is said that he actually fainted the first time he kissed a girl. Her name was

> "Boxing kept me out of trouble."[4]

Areatha Swint and she thought Cassius was joking when he fell down after they kissed. She had to get him a cold cloth. When Cassius recovered he told her he was fine, but he doubted anyone would believe what had happened.[5]

Cassius began attending Central High School in 1957, starting in the tenth grade. He had not improved as a student. His grades were extremely poor. The only subjects he passed were art and gym.

"He was not a good student. School was something he did because he was supposed to," said Bettie Johnson, a counselor at Central High at that time.[6]

Yet the principal, Atwood Wilson, became Cassius's friend and champion. He admired the young man's dedication to his training, even though Wilson would have preferred it if the boy did not spend his time daydreaming in class or going into the bathroom to box in front of the mirror. Cassius fought only in the ring, and Wilson knew this. But he liked to tease the students over the intercom that if anyone acted up, "I'm going to set Cassius Clay on you!"[7]

Cassius continued to push himself. There was another boxing gym in the area, at the Grace Community Center, and it was run by a trainer named Fred Stoner. Cassius saw that Stoner was turning out more—and better—boxers than Joe Martin. Yet Martin did not allow his boys to train at Stoner's gym. Taking a chance, Cassius went with his brother, Rudy, to Stoner's gym one night. There was very little heat in the basement, and the equipment was not as good as Martin's.

Stoner recognized Cassius from the television show *Tomorrow's Champions*. He told Cassius that he had courage and determination but little skill. Stoner invited Cassius to train at his gym at night.

When Martin found out that Cassius had visited Stoner's gym, he gave Cassius a choice: If he wanted to continue fighting for Martin, he could not go to Stoner's gym. Cassius agreed not to train there.

It was a hard promise to keep. Cassius was determined to become not just the best boxer he was capable of being, but the best boxer in the world. He wanted to get the highest level of training possible. He wound up going back to Stoner's from eight to twelve at night. If Martin knew, he did not stop him. Cassius told Stoner, "I'm going to train harder. I want to know everything you can teach me."[8]

He continued training at Martin's gym from six to eight at night, then headed over to Stoner's. He also worked in the afternoons at a Catholic school, dusting the stairs and cleaning the floors.

Training was strenuous at Stoner's gym. Cassius later said

> Cassius wanted to become the best boxer in the world.

that his style and system of boxing originated there. He had to shoot two hundred left jabs—short, quick punches—in a row. If he got tired, he had to start all over again with the first jab. Then he repeated the jabs with his right hand. Cassius was taught how to block a punch and how to shoot right crosses. Each day, he did a hundred push-ups and a hundred knee bends.

Cassius continued working with both Martin and Stoner. Fred Stoner told Cassius that he was not only quick but talented. With hard work, he would come out on top. "You think I can win the Golden Gloves?" Cassius asked, referring to the amateur boxing award.

"Not only the Golden Gloves, you'll take the Olympic Gold Medal in Rome," Stoner replied.[9]

Getting in Shape

Cassius was only a teenager, yet he was training like a professional. He got up before dawn, put on his sweat-suit, and went for a run. He traveled—along with other boys—to tournaments in Chicago, Illinois; Indianapolis, Indiana; and Toledo, Ohio. Joe Martin's wife, Christine, drove the boys. During these trips, the other boys would stare out the windows of the station wagon and whistle at girls walking down the sidewalk. Not Cassius. Christine Martin said that Cassius sat quietly reading the Bible he always carried around with him.[10]

At seventeen, Cassius had as much confidence in himself as Stoner did. Although he was an amateur, Cassius wanted to spar with light-heavyweight boxer Willie Pastrano, who had come to Louisville for a fight. Pastrano's trainer, Angelo Dundee, did not want the two boxers to spar. Pastrano was a professional, and Dundee worried that he might hurt the teenager. But Cassius would not give up. He waited in the gym every day, pestering Dundee and constantly asking if he could work with Pastrano.

> "You think I can win the Golden Gloves?"

Finally, Dundee gave in. Cassius and Pastrano went two rounds. Cassius was unbelievably quick. He always seemed able to hit Pastrano when he least expected it. As the two emerged from the ring, Pastrano told his trainer, "The kid beat the hell out of me."[11]

Dundee agreed. "Willie was a professional on his way to winning the light-heavyweight championship of the world," he said. "And I gotta tell you, Cassius won that round."[12]

Cassius turned eighteen in 1960. He was scheduled to graduate from Central High, but some of the teachers were against allowing him to get a diploma. His school-work and grades had been poor. The teachers believed it would send the wrong message to the students and coaches if Cassius was given special treatment and allowed to grad-uate just because he was an excellent athlete. But principal

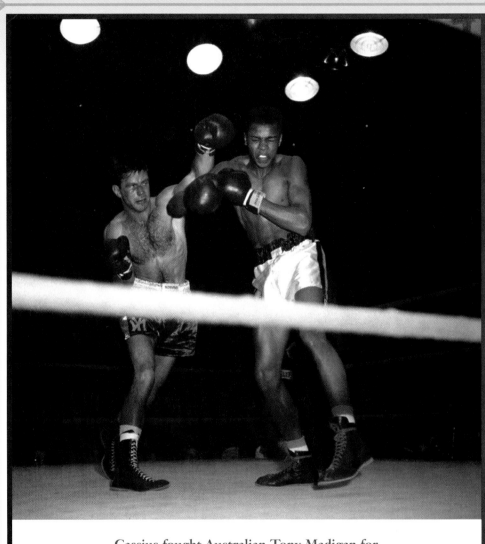

Cassius fought Australian Tony Madigan for
a Golden Gloves championship in 1959.

Atwood Wilson disagreed. He said he would not allow Cassius to fail in his school.

"One day our greatest claim to fame is going to be that we knew Cassius Clay or taught him," said Wilson. "Do you think I'm going to be the principal of a school that Cassius Clay didn't finish?"[13]

Ranked number 376 out of 391 students, Cassius received a certificate of attendance in June 1960. He was a poor reader and always would be. Later in life, he would have to ask his friends to read out loud the newspaper articles that were written about him.

By the time Ali finished high school, he had won six Kentucky Golden Gloves championships, along with two national championships—the National AAU light heavyweight and the Golden Gloves heavyweight. He had an overall record of one hundred wins and just eight losses. Next, he set his sights on the Olympics.

Chapter 4

Going for the Gold

Not long before the 1960 Olympics, Clay was in New York City talking to Dick Schaap, the sports editor of *Newsweek* magazine. Although Schaap was not planning to attend the Olympics in Rome, he had arranged to meet with Clay and another hot boxing prospect, Wilbert "Skeeter" McClure from Toledo, Ohio. Schaap wanted to talk to some of America's best contenders for medals in Rome.

Schaap asked the two boxers if they would like to meet Sugar Ray Robinson. Robinson had captured the middleweight championship five times between 1951 and 1958 and was almost unbeatable during his long career. As a boxer, he was known for his grace and power.

Clay was very enthusiastic about meeting Robinson. For years he had admired the fighter's quick, light boxing style. He also admired Robinson's life of luxury—particularly the fancy pink and purple Cadillacs he bought for himself every year.

Clay, Schaap, and McClure went to Robinson's bar in Harlem, a black neighborhood in the city. While they waited for Robinson, they ate dinner and walked around Harlem. Clay was surprised to see an African-American man standing on a wooden crate, preaching that black people should stand up for their rights. In a racially segregated state like Kentucky, a black man would not have been allowed to make such a speech. But Schaap told Clay that here, the man would not get into trouble.

When Sugar Ray Robinson finally drove up in a purple Cadillac, Clay dropped the arrogant attitude he usually displayed to people. He was in awe of Robinson and stared at him wide-eyed. But Robinson spent only a couple of minutes with the young boxers before moving past them and going into his bar. Later, Clay remembered how hurt he had felt by Robinson's lack of interest in him. "I said to myself right then, 'If I ever get great and famous and people want my autograph enough to wait all day to see me, I'm sure going to treat 'em different,'" Clay said.[1]

Fame was waiting right around the corner for Clay as he got ready for the Olympics. He first had to prove himself at the Olympic trials, which were held at the Cow Palace in San Francisco, California. Clay was his usual self—bragging endlessly about his accomplishments and how he would one day be the greatest boxer in the world.

> Fame was waiting right around the corner for Clay.

The crowd at the Cow Palace did not care for his boasting. They booed Clay when he took to the ring.

Although he was only eighteen, Clay had a lot of experience. He found himself in the final round against Allen Hudson, the U.S. Army champion. Hudson hit hard with his left hand. After two rounds, the fight was fairly even. In the third, Clay pulled himself out of a clinch and delivered a right cross to Hudson's jaw. Hudson wobbled and Clay took advantage of the other boxer's weakness. He hit him until the referee had to stop the match. Clay had won. The 178-pound boxer would travel to Rome with the U.S. Olympic Boxing team as a light heavyweight.

There was only one problem—Clay was afraid of flying. He flatly told Joe Martin that he would not get on the plane that would take him across the Atlantic Ocean to Italy. Martin sat down with Clay and talked to him for several hours. He told Clay that if he ever hoped to become the heavyweight champion of the world, he had to get on the plane, go to Rome, and win the Olympics.

Although Clay finally agreed, he was not happy. He bought a parachute at an army surplus store and wore it on the plane. Martin's son, Joe Jr., said that Clay became so nervous during the rough flight that he got down in the aisle—still wearing his parachute—and prayed.[2]

Clay loved the Olympics. He enjoyed meeting people

and talking nonstop about how he was going to become the Olympic champion. *Sports Illustrated* magazine agreed with Clay, calling him America's best chance for a gold medal in boxing. Floyd Patterson, the current heavyweight champion, came to Rome to see the Olympics. He showed up at the ring to see Clay fight. Clay excitedly told the heavyweight champion that one day he was going to "whup" him.[3] Patterson smiled at the teenaged boxer.

Clay had been serious about boxing since he was twelve. Six years later, he was even more serious about coming away from the Olympics as a champion. "I don't know of anybody on any team who took it more seriously than he did," said McClure, Clay's roommate in Rome. "He worked for that gold medal. . . . When I watched him train, he was one of the hardest trainers I'd ever seen."[4]

Nineteen countries entered contestants in the light-heavyweight division. Clay's first opponent, Yvon Because of Belgium, was tall and thin, and Clay's combination punches were too much for him. Clay won in the second round. He then fought Gennadily Shatkov, a Russian. Clay won this match as well, out-jabbing Shatkov. Now extremely confident, Clay faced Australian Tony Madigan. The two men had fought the year before in Chicago, Illinois, when Clay had won the national Golden Gloves title. Again Clay came away with the victory.

Clay's opponent in the final round was Zbigniew Piertrzkowski, the Polish champion. Piertrzkowski, who

Boxing Terms

Knockout—When a boxer is knocked down and does not get up within ten seconds.

Technical Knockout—When a boxer is judged by the referee to be physically unable to continue fighting.

Decision—When two boxers fight the full number of rounds, but no one has been knocked down. The judges—usually three people—decide the winner. The decision is *unanimous* when everyone agrees, or it is *split* when one judge disagrees.

Weight Divisions—*Lightweight* boxers cannot weigh more than 135 pounds; *welterweight* boxers no more than 147 pounds; *middleweight* boxers no more than 160 pounds; *light heavyweight* boxers no more than 175 pounds; *heavyweight* boxers usually weigh more than 190 pounds, but there is no limit.

was left-handed, had fought more than 230 matches and won a bronze medal at the 1956 Olympics. At first, Clay had some trouble with Piertrzkowski. He found it harder fighting left-handers because their stance was different. Yet he came into his own in the middle of the second round. Clay hit hard and quickly. He was too much for his opponent, who ran from him and hung against the ropes with blood pouring from his face. For the final minute of the round, Piertrzkowski had barely been able to defend himself. The judges awarded the decision to Clay. He had won the gold medal and was now the world's best amateur boxer in the light-heavyweight division.

Clay did not take off his medal for weeks. A friend from the Olympics—Wilma Rudolph, the U.S. sprinter who won three Olympic gold medals in Rome—said that Clay ate with the medal and slept with it hanging around his neck. Clay later said he had to learn to sleep on his back or the medal would have cut his chest.

When Clay flew home, it seemed as if his dreams had come true. He was greeted, he said, with a "hero's welcome."[5] A twenty-five-car motorcade with a police escort rode through Louisville until it reached Clay's high school. There were banners, cheerleaders, and speeches to honor the man who had been predicting his own greatness since he was twelve.

Principal Atwood Wilson, who had made sure Clay finished Central High, announced that Clay was a "fine ambassador" for the country to have sent to Italy.[6] The mayor of Louisville, Bruce Hoblitzell, said that Clay was an inspiration to the young people of the city.

Some weeks later, Clay—who never tired of being the center of attention—decided to drive through the streets. He yelled out from the car that he was the best, the greatest. Wilma Rudolph was visiting from Tennessee, and Clay made

> Clay did not take off his medal for weeks.

Three proud U.S. boxers wear their Olympic gold medals in Rome, 1960.
From left: Wilbert McClure, light middleweight;
Cassius Clay, light heavyweight; and Edward Crook, middleweight.

her accompany him and stand up in the car, too. Rudolph objected at first but finally gave in and stood up. She waved and quickly sat down.

Clay basked in his celebrity status after the Olympics. Yet these were dark times as well, and winning a gold medal could do nothing to change that. When Clay went into a restaurant one day in Louisville with a friend, the owner refused to serve the two African Americans. Clay reached for the gold medal that was always hanging from his neck and held it out. Still, the owner would not serve Clay or his friend.

Now that he had captured the top prize at the Olympics, Clay was planning to make the jump from amateur boxing to professional. Hiring a trainer, paying for equipment, and traveling to fights would cost money. Clay needed financial backing and a manager.

At first, it looked as if William Reynolds, a Louisville businessman who had made a fortune in aluminum, would be the man behind Clay's career. Clay had known Reynolds briefly when he took a job on Reynolds' estate doing yardwork one summer in high school. Reynolds's package called for Joe Martin to continue as Clay's trainer. Reynolds's lawyer put together the deal, which called for Clay to receive a salary along with additional money that would be put into a bank account for Clay to use later. Clay and his parents agreed to the terms initially and then, suddenly, decided not to go through with it.

Clay's father was against the agreement because he was uncomfortable that Martin was included. Not only had Martin never trained a professional fighter, he was a policeman—and a white policeman at that. Cassius Clay Sr. had been arrested enough times to be wary of the police. The deal was off.

William Faversham Jr., an actor and vice president of Brown-Forman Distillers, approached the Clay family.

Along with several other businessmen, Faversham put together the Louisville Sponsoring Group. It was made up of eleven wealthy men from around Kentucky: Patrick Calhoun Jr. bred horses and had once been chairman of the American Commercial Barge Line. Vertner DeGarmo Smith was a former sales manager for Brown-Forman. William Sol Cutchins headed Brown & Williamson Tobacco. Elbert Gary Sutcliffe invested heavily in U.S. Steel. William Lee Lyons Brown was chairman of the board for

This waitress has refused to serve her black customer. Even after Clay became an Olympic champ, he could not avoid the hateful realities of segregation.

Brown-Forman. Robert Worth Bingham was in the publishing business. George Washington Norton IV served as secretary-treasurer of WAVE-TV, the station that showed *Tomorrow's Champions*. J. D. Stetson Coleman headed an oil company in Oklahoma along with other businessmen. Archibald McGhee Foster helped run a New York advertising agency. James Ross Todd had his money invested in several businesses.

They were all white, all wealthy, and for the most part knew practically nothing about boxing. They hoped that investing in Clay would be profitable as well as entertaining. Each sponsor put in $2,800, except Faversham, who contributed only $1,400 because he was the organizer.

Clay received a $10,000 bonus when he signed the contract. With the money, Clay bought a used Cadillac for his parents. He also received a guaranteed salary of $4,800—or $200 a month—for the first two years. Any money Clay made inside or outside the boxing ring was to be divided up evenly between the syndicate and Clay for the first four years. After that time, Clay would receive 60 percent of the earnings, with the other 40 percent going to the syndicate. The syndicate would pay for all training, traveling, management, and promotional expenses. Plus, 15 percent of Clay's earnings would go into a pension fund. He would not be able to touch this money until he was thirty-five years old or had retired from boxing.

Faversham was to be the manager of the Louisville

Sponsoring Group. It fell on his shoulders to decide where Clay would box and against which opponents. Clay was eager to make his professional debut. He got his chance on October 29, 1960, one month after he had won his Olympic medal. He was set to fight in Louisville against Tunney Hunsaker from Fayetteville, West Virginia. Hunsaker had a 17–8 record. He was a large man and not terribly quick. "He kept me away from him," said Hunsaker later.[7]

Clay won the decision after a six-round fight. "He was fast as lightning," Hunsaker said of Clay, "and he could hit from any position without getting hit. I tried just about every trick I knew to throw him off balance, but he was just too good."[8]

Even so, Clay had not knocked out Hunsaker. Faversham and the Louisville Sponsoring Group did not think Clay's first performance as a professional was impressive. They decided he should spend some time at Archie Moore's boxing camp in California.

Moore, who was the light-heavyweight champion at that time, ran a training camp about thirty-five miles from San Diego in the city of Ramona. Clay's sponsors believed Moore's experience would help guide their young boxer in the right direction. Although Moore was forty-seven, he was still fighting and was something of a legend.

Clay liked the appearance of Moore's gym. It was called Bucket of Blood and had a painting of a skull on the

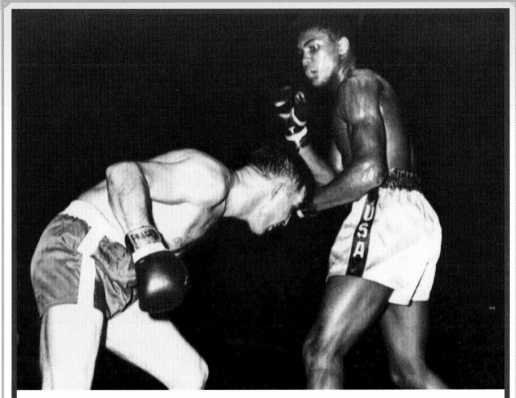

Six thousand fans watched Clay's first fight as a professional boxer. His opponent was Tunney Hunsaker, a part-time fighter and full-time West Virginia police chief.

front door. The names of some famous boxers were painted on boulders that stood outside: Joe Louis, Ray Robinson, Jack Johnson.

Moore also liked what he saw in the young boxer. Clay had incredible stamina and discipline. Twice, he ran up a steep hill and then asked Moore if he should do it again.

Clay was not only determined, he was loaded with talent. Yet when Moore wanted to teach him how to knock a man out in only one or two rounds, Clay was not interested. Even when Moore explained that Clay would last longer as a boxer this way and be able to fight for many years, Clay said no. He did not want to be like Moore, still fighting in his forties, he said. He told Moore that he wanted to fight for only five or six years. Once he had made $2 million to $3 million, he planned to quit, get married, and raise a family.

The only part of training camp that Clay strongly disliked was helping with chores. Moore did not have a staff, so the boxers had to wash dishes, chop wood for the stove, scrub floors, cook meals, and do other odd jobs. "I didn't come here to be a dishwasher," Clay said.[9] He did the work, but there was no doubt as to how he felt about it.

By December, it was clear the arrangement was not going to work out. The men liked each other, but Clay insisted on having things his own way. It was very difficult for Moore to teach him. Clay took a train home before Christmas and did not return to Moore's gym.

His sponsors were not upset by the turn of events. Although Moore's training camp had not been the right place for Clay, they knew he was a dedicated boxer. What they needed to find now was a trainer. Faversham called up Harry Markson, president of MSG Boxing, and asked his advice. Markson told him to get Angelo Dundee.[10]

Chapter 5

Training and Fighting

ngelo Dundee already knew Clay from their meeting a few years earlier. He readily accepted a salary of $125 a week to train the young boxer. Although Dundee wanted to start after Christmas, Clay was anxious to begin immediately. As usual, Clay got what he wanted. He began training with Dundee on December 19, 1960.

Nearly everyone in the boxing world had a high regard for Dundee. He was considered a decent and honest man. A native of Philadelphia, Dundee worked with Hall of Fame boxer Carmen Basilio, who had captured both the welterweight and middleweight titles, plus various other world championships. As a trainer, Dundee was known for being an excellent motivator and a quick thinker. He ran the Miami Beach Fifth Street Gym in Florida. Along with rats and termites, the gym had plywood floors, speed bags

Angelo Dundee

and heavy bags, several tables for rubdowns, and not much more. The place was lit by a few plain light bulbs.

Clay stayed at a cheap hotel in a poor Miami neighborhood. Although he occasionally went to nightclubs—sometimes just standing outside to listen to the music—Clay never drank anything except orange juice and he would not stay out late. He liked getting up at five in the morning and going for a run. He also liked Dundee and soon considered him a friend. Clay appreciated that Dundee always treated him with respect and never tried to boss him around.

Clay was interested in two things: training and fighting. His weight soon jumped from 189 pounds to more than 200 pounds—and it was solid muscle. Dundee never had to push Clay to work hard. "It was like jet propulsion," he said. "Just touch him and he took off."[1]

Dundee quickly found out what Archie Moore had realized. It was practically impossible to tell Clay to do anything. The young boxer was determined to fight his own way. So when Dundee made suggestions to Clay, he worded them so that it seemed as if the ideas were actually Clay's. For example, Dundee might compliment Clay on the placement of his left knee as he jabbed. Clay might not have been placing his knee in any particular way, but the next time he went out, he would pay attention to it. "But mainly, it was all him," said Dundee. "His quickness, the ability to get in and get out, was unbelievable from the start."[2]

In February 1961, former heavyweight champion Ingemar Johansson came to Miami to fight the current champion, Floyd Patterson. Johansson needed partners to spar with. When Clay was asked if he would be interested, he said, "I'll go dancin' with Johansson."[3]

Johansson, in his late twenties, had been born in Göteborg, Sweden. He had won the silver medal in the 1952 Olympic Games. Johansson became the heavyweight champion seven years later, when he took the title from Patterson in only three rounds. However, Patterson knocked out Johansson a year later, taking back the heavyweight title. Johansson was now preparing for a third match with Patterson.

First Johansson had to spar with Clay—and he was no match for the young boxer. Clay moved quickly around Johansson, hitting him with constant left jabs in his face, which Johansson seemed unable to prevent. And Clay never stopped talking while he went to work. He made fun of Johansson, insulting him and bragging that he—Clay—should be the one facing Patterson.

After two rounds, Johansson was exhausted and his trainer stopped the fight. Clay was moving up in the boxing world. He had fought four professional matches, and in a sparring match had just beaten the man who recently held the heavyweight title.

Clay next fought Donnie Fleeman. Fleeman was tough, but Clay's quickness was too much for the Texan. When Clay took on heavyweight Lamar Clark in his hometown of Louisville, he bragged that he would win the fight in two rounds. Clark had forty-five knockouts in a row to his credit, but Clay lived up to his words. During the second round, he broke Clark's nose. Clark fell twice, and the match was over.

It took Clay longer to prevail over Duke Sabedong. After ten rounds, the decision went to Clay. This fight took place in Las Vegas, Nevada. While Clay was there, he went on a radio show with professional wrestler Gorgeous George. George was so loud and brash that he made Clay seem silent. George screamed and raved about everything he planned to do to his opponent. He threatened to kill the opponent and rip his arms off. Most importantly, George gave Clay some advice the nineteen-year-old boxer never forgot: Talking draws a crowd. "A lot of people will pay to see someone shut your mouth," George said.[4]

Clay spent the next year fighting a number of heavyweights, including Alonzo Johnson, Alex Miteff, Willie

Besmanoff, Sonny Banks, Don Warner, George Logan, Billy Daniels, and Alejandro Lavorante. Clay won every match. He was quick, he hit hard, and he was relentless. "He'll pick you and peck you, peck you and pick you, until you don't know where you are," said Harry Wiley, Banks's cornerman.[5] The cornerman is the person who attends to a boxer between rounds.

As 1962 drew to a close, Clay found himself in the ring with his old trainer from California, Archie Moore. At

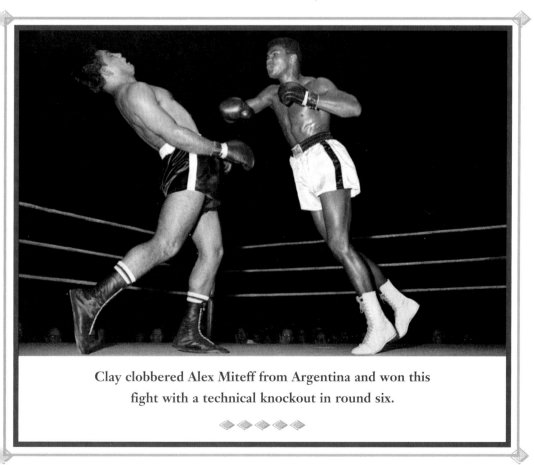

Clay clobbered Alex Miteff from Argentina and won this fight with a technical knockout in round six.

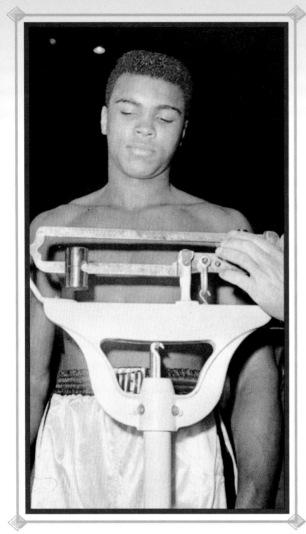

Clay weighs in before a match in 1962.

❖ ❖ ❖ ❖ ❖

forty-eight, Moore was more than twice Clay's age and certainly not in the best shape. He hoped that Clay's inexperience would cause him to make a mistake. Clay had no intention of making a mistake and boasted that he would dispose of Moore after four rounds.

Clay was in control as soon as the fight began. Although Moore had once been known for his accuracy and punching power, these skills had long since disappeared. Clay jabbed at Moore's head—and kept jabbing. Moore got in one good shot in the second round, but that was it. True to his word, Clay won the match in four rounds.

He kept winning. On January 24, 1963, he fought Charlie Powell, who used to play professional football. Powell taunted Clay before the match, and Clay became angry. But he managed to keep his cool in the ring, and he won the match after three rounds.

One of Clay's toughest matches was against Doug Jones in March 1963 at New York City's Madison Square Garden. Because the newspapers were on strike at that time, Clay ran around drumming up publicity for the match on radio and television. By the day of the fight, he was tired. He had posed for pictures and appeared on talk shows until he was worn out.

The fight was not one of his best. Jones, with experience on his side, was able to duck away from Clay's jabs and counter-punches. Throughout the match, it was not certain Clay would win. It went the full ten rounds and eventually the decision went to Clay. When the decision was announced, many of the spectators were upset and threw peanuts, beer cups, and cigar stubs toward the ring. Clay picked up a few peanuts, shelled them, and ate them. Then he lifted his arms in victory. But it had been close, and Clay knew it.

Journalists for newspapers and sports magazines came down hard on Clay. In spite of the victory, his poor show-ing against Jones made many people wonder if he needed more substance behind the bragging. When he had won decisively, the boasting had been amusing. Now, they said, it was becoming annoying.

Three months after the Jones match, Clay was in London, set to fight Henry Cooper, Britain's heavyweight

His Strongest Weapon

Although he kept winning, Clay was criticized. Some boxing experts claimed he performed his quick dancing movements around the ring to avoid getting hit. As for his jabs, the experts complained that they were not hard enough. But Dundee maintained that the only reason a boxer gets hit is that he is unable to get out of the way. No one wants to get hit. It was to Clay's credit that he nearly always seemed to be able to keep away from the punches. Clay managed to aim his jabs in such a way that his opponents were stunned or at least cut. "He was a marksman with his jab," Dundee said.[6] Clay himself said his strongest weapon as a young fighter was his legs. They were strong, quick, and incredibly well conditioned. He would dance around the other boxer, managing to keep just out of range, until he could get in a punch and move out again.

champion. Entering the ring wearing a crown of imitation jewels, Clay predicted the match would go no more than five rounds. After three rounds, Cooper was weak and ready to go down. His face was covered in blood from a cut above one eye. Yet suddenly—in the fourth round—he landed a left hook on Clay's jaw and the young boxer fell backward through the ropes. He quickly got back into the ring and looked shaky. As he began to fall, Clay was caught

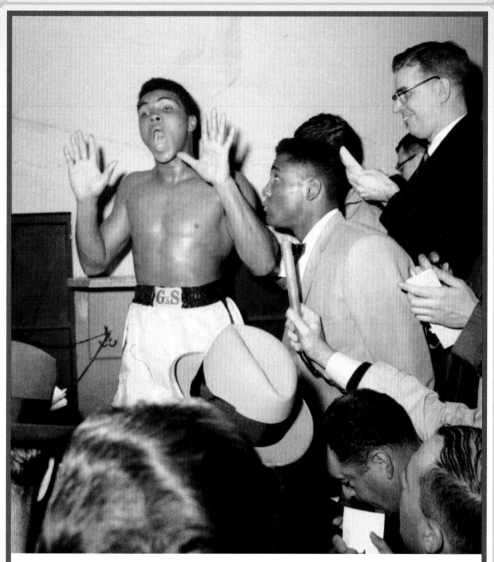

Even after his lackluster victory over Doug Jones in 1963,
Clay was full of his usual bravado. Photographers often caught Clay
with his mouth wide open, boasting about his skills.

by his handlers. He stood dazed as the fourth round ended. His cornermen iced his back and Dundee gave him smelling salts. Clay was hurt and he needed to be revived.

When the fifth round began, Clay fought as if he had never been injured. His first jab cut Cooper's eye "as a cleaver would have," wrote Robert Daley of *The New York Times*.[7] He continued with a barrage of punches aimed at Cooper's head that resulted in the Englishman bleeding profusely. Cooper was being beaten in the truest sense of the word. The crowd screamed for the referees to stop the fight. And just as Clay had predicted, after five rounds, they did. "I'm the boldest, the prettiest, the most superior, most scientific, most skillfullest fighter in the ring today," Clay crowed.[8]

To prove he was everything he claimed to be, Clay knew that he now had to fight Sonny Liston, heavyweight champion of the world.

Chapter 6

The Greatest

C harles "Sonny" Liston was a scary man. He had been put in prison twice—once for armed robbery and a second time for assaulting a policeman. He was a big man who hit hard and looked as if nothing could destroy him.

When Liston was serving time in prison in 1952 on the robbery charge, a priest realized that the twenty-year-old had boxing talent. Liston left prison that October and spent less than a year boxing as an amateur.

He moved into professional boxing in September 1953. Liston did not lose a fight until he came up against Marty Marshall. Although he lost to Marshall in an eight-round decision, Liston went on to beat Marshall in a rematch in 1955.

Forced to spend six months in jail in 1957 for beating up a policeman, Liston returned to boxing the following year. He won eight fights in 1958 and four fights—all of them knockouts—in 1959. He won five more in 1960. Sonny Liston was the most feared man in the boxing world.

After another arrest that resulted in the temporary suspension of his boxing license, Liston fought Floyd Patterson for the world heavyweight title on September 25, 1962. The fight was held at Comiskey Park in Chicago, Illinois. It took Liston two minutes and six seconds to become the new world champion. He knocked out Patterson in the first round. A rematch between the two men nearly a year later had the same result—Liston knocked out Patterson in the first round. This time, it took two minutes and ten seconds. Some boxing experts thought Liston was the greatest heavyweight champion that had ever lived.

"Virtually no one thought that Cassius Clay had a chance to beat Sonny Liston," said Thomas Hauser, author of several books on boxing. "Certainly Sonny Liston didn't. Sonny Liston was one of the scariest presences on the sporting scene ever."[1]

If Clay had drawn attention to himself in the past for his loud, boastful words, it was nothing compared to his verbal attack on Liston before the fight. As soon as Liston arrived in Miami to begin training, Clay made sure he was always around him, mouthing off.

"It's my time to howl
Rumble, man, rumble
Float like a butterfly
Sting like a bee
Your hands can't hit what your eyes can't see."[2]

He called Liston a "big, ugly bear" and yelled that he was going to go bear hunting.[3] Clay shouted in Liston's face that he was only a chump and that Clay was the true champ. Liston was not amused. More than once, he threatened to hurt Clay if Clay did not stop.

But the constant heckling was part of Clay's plan. He knew he had taken on a lot when he had asked to fight Liston. The man was champion of the world, and Clay had more than a few concerns about the outcome of the fight. So, hoping to intimidate Liston (or at least give him something to worry about), Clay decided he would harass him. "I figured Liston would get so mad that, when the fight came, he'd try to kill me and forget everything he knew about boxing."[4]

> The constant heckling was part of Clay's plan.

Clay also had a plan for inside the ring. Even though he trained extremely hard, Clay knew that no fighter could give 100 percent for fifteen rounds. He aimed to keep from getting hit during the first two rounds. By the third round, Liston would begin to grow tired. Clay would let Liston wear himself out for the next few rounds

LISTON		AGE		CLAY
29		AGE		22
220		WEIGHT		215
		HEIGHT		
6 ft. 1 in.				6 ft. 3 in.
		REACH		
84 in.				82 in.
		CHEST NORMAL		
44 in.				42 in.
		CHEST EXPANDED		
46 ½ in.				44 ½ in.
		WAIST		
36 in.				34 in.
		THIGH		
25 in.				25 in.
		FIST		
15 ½ in.				12 in.
		NECK		
17 ½ in.				17 in.
		BICEPS		
17 ½ in.				15 in..

Was Clay ready to take on the fearsome Sonny Liston?

while Clay conserved his own energy. Then, in the sixth round, Clay would give it all he had, until the fight was over. And *that*, Clay predicted, would happen in the eighth round.

The plan made sense. Liston trained . . . but only half-heartedly. He did not think he needed to worry about endurance. Liston was confident he could beat this twenty-two-year-old kid whom he did not view as an equal.

He was not alone in thinking this.

Billy Conn, former light-heavyweight champion, said of Clay before the fight, "The first punch Liston hits him, out he goes. He can't fight now and he'll never be able to fight. He hasn't the experience. The only experience he'll get with Liston is how to get killed in a hurry."[5]

So Liston jumped rope, hit punching bags, and ran one or two miles a few times a week. But he also ate junk food and drank beer.

The weigh-in took place on the morning of February 25, 1964. Keeping up his antics, Clay walked into the room wearing a jacket that had "Bear Huntin'" written across the back. He screamed and shouted, lunging toward Liston. "Float like a butterfly, sting like a bee!" he yelled. "This is it, you big ugly bear!"[6]

Los Angeles Times boxing writer Jim Murray said that Clay "went beserk" at the weigh-in. "He was shouting and screaming and we all thought it was fear. Because the classic defense against fear is noise."[7]

Many people thought Clay was terrified. Even the doctor who took Clay's pulse—and found it more than twice the normal rate—believed it was probably because Clay was scared. Finding Clay's blood pressure reading to be equally high, the doctor said there would be no fight that evening unless Clay calmed down. Yet Clay's "hysteria" was an act. "I've rehearsed and planned every move I make that day," he said.[8] Clay wanted Liston to think he was hysterical, "crazy." "Liston has been boasting he's afraid of no man alive," said Clay. "But Liston means no sane man—Liston's got to be afraid of a crazy man."[9]

> Clay wanted Liston to think he was hysterical, "crazy."

Clay went early to the ring to see his brother, Rudy—also a heavyweight—fight. He shouted encouraging words to Rudy, who eventually won the match by decision even though he had been considerably bruised.

As the time of the Liston-Clay fight approached, about half the seats in the arena filled up with people. Only 8,297 tickets had been sold in an arena that could hold 15,744. The tickets were expensive and no one expected it to be much of a fight. Liston was heavily favored—seven to one. Liston himself was confident while Clay was, in fact, nervous. "I won't lie; I was scared," said Clay later. "Sonny Liston was one of the greatest fighters of all time. . . . He hit hard; and he was fixing to kill me."[10]

The boxers came into the ring at 10 P.M. and Liston

stared at Clay, trying to frighten him. Trainer Angelo Dundee told Clay to stand tall, so Liston would see that he was fighting a man taller than he was. Clay listened; he stared right back at Liston, using every inch of his six-foot-three frame to look down on his opponent.

The bell signaled the start of the first round and Clay began to do what he did best—he moved quickly, lightly, avoiding Liston's jabs and forcing him to hit at nothing. Liston hit hard and he connected with Clay's torso. Yet Clay instantly danced away and Liston was unable to follow up. Liston had never fought anyone who moved like this before. Clay's reflexes were astonishing. He seemed able to avoid Liston's jabs the instant before they landed. Near the end of the round, Clay began jabbing at Liston.

Types of Punches

A jab is a short, straight punch. It is the most important punch because it can hurt the opponent while still leaving you protected. A straight right is a power punch. As your right hand goes out toward your opponent, you are forced to move your weight into the punch. The left (or right) hook is an inside power punch. It is a swinging blow delivered with a crooked arm. The uppercut is a swinging blow that is delivered upward, usually at your opponent's chin.

He landed eight in a row—quick, painful blows that forced Liston to cover up.

The bell sounded, but Clay and Liston kept fighting. The referee came in and separated the men. Clay sat down in his corner. He was no longer nervous. "You won that round and you're going to win the whole thing," Dundee told him.[11]

The second round began and Clay continued to dance around Liston, even as he suffered a few punches. But Clay moved so well that at one point, Liston hit the ropes instead of his opponent. Meanwhile, Clay began to concentrate his jabs under Liston's eyes.

The onslaught continued in the third round. A cut under Liston's eye was bleeding, as was his nose. Clay kept attacking the eye and by the end of the round, Liston's face was full of blood.

Boxing historian Bert Sugar said it was incredible to watch what was happening to the fearsome Liston. "This . . . underdog was outrunning him, outgunning him, and shaming him," said Sugar.[12]

Clay planned to take it easy in the fourth round. He needed time to give his body a break and gather his energy for the remainder of his fight. He ran Liston around, hoping to wear him out. Yet as the round drew to a close, Clay's eyes suddenly began to sting. He felt a burning, needle-like pain, and nearly blind, he clawed at his face.

"I can't see!" he yelled. "Cut off the gloves!"[13]

The round ended with Clay screaming in pain. "I didn't care if it was a heavyweight title fight I had worked so long for," he said, "I wasn't going out there and get murdered because I couldn't see."[14]

Dundee stayed calm. He touched the corner of Clay's eye with his pinky. Dundee then touched the pinky to his own eye. He felt a burning, stinging pain and realized that an ointment used to treat boxers' cuts had somehow gotten into Clay's eyes. Dundee did not want Clay to give up on the match. He took a sponge and rinsed Clay's eyes out numerous times with cool water. While he did this, he kept encouraging Clay to go out there and fight.

"This is the big one. This is for the title shot," said Dundee. "You gotta go back out there. You're winning."[15]

As the bell sounded, Clay resumed the fight with his right eye closed. Although he could barely see, Clay managed to duck Liston's blows and move swiftly away from him, just out of reach. Round five continued, and by the end, Clay's eyes began to clear.

> "This is the big one. This is for the title shot."

"I could see again," he said, "and I was ready to carry the fight to Liston. And I was gaining my second wind now, as I had conditioned myself, to pace the fight.[16]

He had been hit by Liston, but not severely enough to do any serious damage. Liston was tired. He had never thought the fight would last this long.

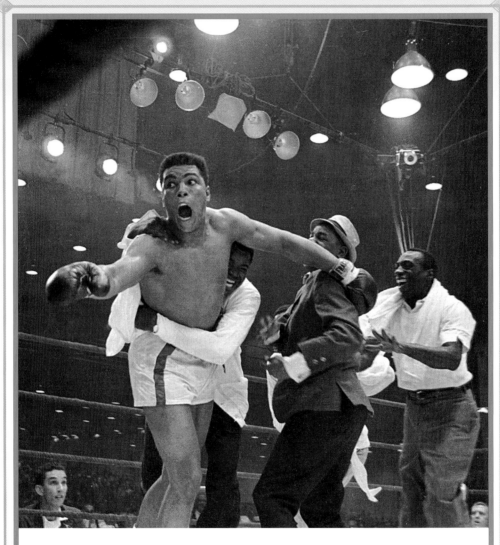

"I'm king of the world!" roared Clay after
winning the heavyweight title in 1964.

The bell sounded for round six, and Clay was himself again. He was able to see clearly, and he had a surge of energy. Standing practically flat-footed, he began to punch Liston, hitting him with a left hook and right uppercuts. Liston doubled up as Clay jabbed at the deep cut under Liston's eye. He jabbed Liston sharply in the head twice, snapping back his opponent's head.

The round ended and Liston sat on his stool in the corner. "That's it," he said.[17] His cornermen thought he said the words as a challenge. He had put up with enough. Now he would go out there and really show Clay who the heavyweight champion of the world was.

But Liston would not move. He was tired and hurt. He refused to continue fighting.

Meanwhile, Clay was waiting for the start of round seven. Then he saw Liston spit out his mouthpiece and realized he was not getting up from his stool. Clay leaped around the ring with his arms over his head.

"I told you," Clay screamed to reporters and anyone who would listen, "I told you—I am the greatest."[18]

Chapter 7

A New Direction

C lay had boasted often enough that he was the greatest . . . and now he was. The question many people asked was, "Why?" First, Clay was a large man. He was nearly six feet three inches tall and had a long reach, which helped Clay keep his opponents away from him. He held his hands low, allowing him to punch directly at a shorter opponent rather than hitting down, which could often be difficult. His muscular shoulders and chest were the basis of his heavy hitting. Clay had strong legs and quick feet as well, and they were the foundation of his power. Although he came by these physical gifts naturally, Clay did everything he could to make the most of them.

Clay was determined to remain in top condition. His training regimen was rigorous. It was this conditioning that allowed him to last through long fights without suffering from exhaustion.

Clay's style of boxing also contributed to his greatness. It was unusual for a large man to be so quick, so light on his feet. Clay had the speed of a lighter, more wiry man. Combined with his reflexes, the result was outstanding.

Clay did not hit like typical heavyweight boxers, most of whom were sluggers. He delivered short, snapping punches. They were extremely effective, especially when one of these karate-style punches landed on an opponent's chin. Some boxing experts criticized Clay's ability to avoid being hit. Yet this strategy allowed an opponent to get tired and frustrated, ultimately

> Clay's style of boxing also contributed to his greatness.

forgetting about defense in a rash effort to deliver one solid knockout punch.

Finally, Clay had the drive to win. "If I were a garbageman, I'd be the world's greatest garbageman!" he said. "I'd pick up more garbage and faster than anyone has ever seen. To tell you the truth, I would have been the world's greatest at whatever I'd done!"[1]

The morning after the Liston fight, Clay appeared at a press conference in Miami Beach. He answered numerous questions about his victory. Clay explained that he had expected to win the fight and he had done so because he was the better boxer.

"I shook up
the world!
I can't
be beat!"[2]

Then one of the reporters asked Clay a question that had nothing to do with boxing. It concerned Clay's religion and his recent conversion to the Nation of Islam. Clay had become close with Elijah Muhammad, leader of the religious movement that is also called the Black Muslims. Clay also spent a lot of time talking to Malcolm X, a black militant leader who was a minister for the Nation of Islam.

Clay knew the Nation of Islam was not popular among white people. The Black Muslims at that time stood in favor of a separate black nation and were suspicious of whites. Many observers believed that the organization promoted racial hatred. Yet Clay's financial backers were white. His trainer was white. The press that covered him was—for the most part—white.

Clay spoke about his membership in the Nation of Islam at the press conference, and he went into more depth for reporters the next day. He said the reason he had become a Black Muslim was that African Americans were treated unfairly in the United States. He said he had watched black men and women get hurt fighting for integration and equal rights. Clay added that even though he had just become heavyweight champion of the world, there were neighborhoods where he could not live because African Americans were not welcome. "I just want

The controversial African-American leader Malcolm X, left,
taught Clay about the Black Muslim religion.

to be happy with my own kind," Clay said. "A man has got to know where he belongs."[3]

A month later, Clay—who had been calling himself Cassius X since joining the Nation of Islam —changed his name to reflect his African identity. He was rejecting his slave heritage and the name of his slave-owning white ancestors. He became Muhammad Ali, which means beloved of God.

Although some people criticized his actions, one of the few people who did not care about Ali's new religious beliefs was his trainer Angelo Dundee. As long as Ali showed up at the gym to train, Dundee had no interest in his religion.

Ali left the United States on May 14, 1964, to take a tour of Africa. He was greeted as a hero when he traveled

From Clay to Ali

Ali received a lot of criticism for joining the Black Muslims. Ed Lassman, president of the World Boxing Association, said Ali's behavior was harmful to the world of boxing and he was setting a bad example for youngsters. Many reporters felt Ali was using his heavyweight title to preach the religion of the Nation of Islam. They continued to refer to him as Cassius Clay in their newspaper articles, refusing to acknowledge his new name.

Ali was very serious about his
commitment to the Nation of Islam.

to Ghana and Egypt. He rode camels, visited the pyramids, and returned home after a month.

By this time, Malcolm X had broken with Elijah Muhammad over differing beliefs. Malcolm X was no longer as strongly in favor of black separatism as he had been in the past. He now considered the possibility of world brotherhood.

Ali saw Malcolm X during his trip to Africa, yet no longer greeted him in a friendly manner. Ali remained faithful to Elijah Muhammad.

The country was changing, and there was a great push by many Americans for social reforms. On July 2, 1964, the Civil Rights Act went into effect. It gave more employment opportunities to African Americans and banned racial discrimination in public places such as restaurants and hotels.

It was during this time that Ali met Sonji Roi, a twenty-three-year-old model and waitress. Although Ali was shy with women, he proposed to Sonji the first night he met her. Little more than a month later, in August 1964, they were married in Gary, Indiana.

Ali now concentrated on a rematch with Liston. The fight was scheduled for November 16, 1964. Again Liston was favored to win. Most people believed Ali had gotten lucky the first time and that Liston had not trained properly for the match. Ali's weight had soared up to 231 and he needed to get back into shape. Training hard, Ali got down to 210 pounds, although he had added two inches to his biceps (arm muscles) and thighs. He was stronger physically and mentally than he had been the first time he fought Liston.

Three days before the match, Ali felt sick. His abdomen hurt and he was nauseated. He began vomiting and went to the hospital. Doctors found that Ali had a hernia: Part of his intestines had pushed through a space in the muscles of his abdomen. He was operated on immediately, and the match had to be postponed six months. The date was re-set for May 25, 1965.

Three months before the fight, Malcolm X was assassinated. His followers believed the assassination had been ordered by Elijah Muhammad. That same evening, a suspicious fire broke out in Ali's apartment, and two days later the New York headquarters of the Nation of Islam was bombed. The boxing promoters were afraid that there would be more violence because of Ali's connection with the Nation of Islam. The fight was moved from its original location in Boston, Massachusetts, to Lewiston, Maine.

Ali was ready. He had recovered and trained hard. The fight was a short one, ending less than two minutes after it began. As the opening bell sounded, Ali caught Liston off guard with a straight right. He followed a minute later with another right. Avoiding Liston's jabs, Ali gave him a final blow to the head, which threw Liston off balance.

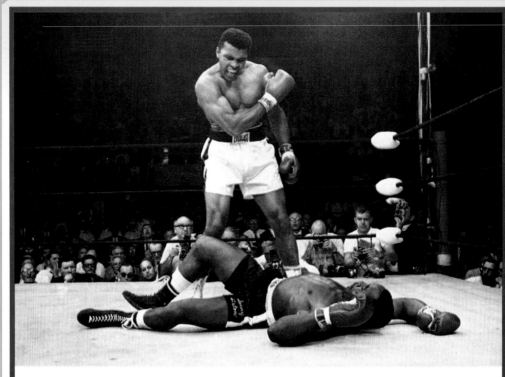

Ali knocked out challenger Liston in 1 minute, 42 seconds, in the first round of their May 1965 fight in Maine.

Liston fell to the floor. The punch was so quick that few people saw it clearly. Ali's arm merely looked like a blur. He was ready to follow up with another punch, but there was no need. Liston stayed on the ground.

In his dressing room afterward, Liston was asked whether he ever saw that final punch. He answered, "Yes, but I saw it too late."[4]

Ali met one more challenger that year—the former heavyweight champion Floyd Patterson. Patterson was determined to beat Ali. He had made a public statement that it was a disgrace to the country and to the world of sports that the heavyweight champ was a Black Muslim.

Patterson was not able to defeat Ali. The November 22 fight lasted twelve rounds. Patterson got a muscle spasm in his back in the third round and was overwhelmed with pain. Yet Ali threw punch after punch and was finally declared the winner. Some boxing experts criticized Ali for allowing the fight to last as long as it did when Patterson was obviously in pain. They claimed he purposely refrained from knocking out Patterson. "That's the way it is," Ali said. "You knock out a guy quickly, as I did Sonny Liston twice, and everybody yells, 'fake.' Then you practice the art of boxing and a man lasts twelve rounds and you're cruel. You can't win."[5]

Ali would soon become involved in a much more serious fight, which had nothing to do with the boxing ring.

Ali was firmly against war. At the draft office, he asked that his name
be taken off the list of people being called to serve in the army.

Chapter 8

Another Kind of Fight

Soon after Ali's victory over Patterson in November 1965, his marriage to Sonji came to an end. Another upheaval came into Ali's life when he learned that he was going to be drafted into the U.S. Army. The news came as a surprise.

Back in 1964, Ali had gone to the Armed Forces Induction Center in Coral Gables, Florida, to take the military qualifying exam. He easily passed the physical part of the test. The mental aptitude test, however, posed many challenges for Ali. Not only was he a poor reader, but he found mathematics to be very difficult. The results of the test revealed that Ali had an army IQ score of seventy-eight. "I said I was the greatest," stated Ali, "not the smartest."[1]

To receive a passing grade, Ali would have had to place in the thirtieth percentile or higher. His score placed him in the sixteenth percentile. He was classified as 1-Y, which meant he was not qualified to serve in the armed forces. Ali was embarrassed by the publicity given to his low test scores. He said he simply did not do well with pencil and paper, "but I've got lots of common sense."[2]

By 1966, with so many men being called to fight in Vietnam, the military lowered its passing-grade requirement. Ali was eligible to be drafted. His draft ranking was changed to A-1, meaning he was very likely to be called into service.

This created a problem for the boxer, who said it went against his conscience to fight in the war, because the Koran, the holy book of the Nation of Islam stated that followers should not kill.[3]

Reporters called Ali, asking repeatedly what he was going to do. After numerous phone calls, Ali lost patience and said, "Man, I ain't got no quarrel with them Vietcong."[4]

His statement became front-page news, and much of the American public blasted him. Many people believed that Ali should fulfill his duty as a United States citizen. They felt other Americans were being drafted—why not Ali? They called him a disgrace.

Ali appealed his A-1 status, but the government refused to change his eligibility. When his name came to the top of the draft list, he would be legally required to report for induction to the army. Until then, he could carry on with his life as a boxer.

Ali was slated to fight Ernie Terrell in Chicago, Illinois, on March 29, 1966. Terrell was heavyweight champion of the World Boxing Association. But Ali's remarks about the army had put the match in jeopardy. Many Chicago newspaper reporters wanted the Illinois State Athletic Commission to cancel the fight. The match was called off.

Conscientious Objector

Ali considered himself a conscientious objector, someone who refuses to serve in the armed forces on grounds of conscience. There were many conscientious objectors during the Vietnam War. A law passed after World War II stated that conscientious objectors could refuse to serve in the army only for religious reasons. In 1970, the Supreme Court took away the religious requirement. People could object based on strong feelings against war and violence. Yet in 1971, the Supreme Court refused to let anyone object to one particular war (which many people were doing because they did not believe the United States should be fighting in Vietnam). Because of this decision, nearly one hundred thousand men fled the United States so that they would not have to be drafted to serve in Vietnam.

The fight promoters now looked at other cities, including Louisville, Kentucky; Miami, Florida; Pittsburgh, Pennsylvania; Bangor, Maine; and Huron, South Dakota. In each city, the fight was banned. Then Ernie Terrell said he would not fight in the match under any conditions. It seemed as if no one wanted anything to do with Muhammad Ali.

Finally, city officials in Toronto, Canada, agreed to let Ali fight there. His opponent was to be Canadian heavyweight champion George Chuvalo. Chuvalo said the atmosphere was strained when Ali arrived in Toronto for the fight. Yet Ali did not seem to be bothered by the outcry against him. Because of the way Chuvalo threw his arm around when he took a swing, Ali called him "the Washerwoman."[5]

> It seemed as if no one wanted anything to do with Ali.

Chuvalo was a well-known and respected name in the world of heavyweight boxing. In 1965, he had fought a match with former heavyweight champion Floyd Patterson. Chuvalo lost the bout but was admired for the courage he displayed.

For his part, Chuvalo planned to be rough with Ali. He intended to fight hard and hurt his opponent, forcing him to quit.

The plan did not work. Chuvalo had won more than fifty fights, but he could not handle Ali. Ali was too quick, handing out an array of jabs, hooks, and uppercuts. Chuvalo did not go down, but after fifteen rounds all three judges gave Ali the win. Two of the judges claimed Ali had lost only one round (the third judge said Ali had lost two rounds).

"I lost the fight," said Chuvalo. "But in a crazy kind of way it made Canadians feel good. . . . I made my fellow Canadians feel proud of being Canadian. And that part makes me feel good, made me feel nice. I can feel proud of that part. . . . That's what people remember me by. So that fight will live forever. . . . No matter where I go it's always the same. 'What a great fight. You fought Muhammad Ali.'"[6]

Ali now traveled through Europe. When he appeared in Sweden for some exhibition matches, his recent ordeal seemed to have taken its toll on him. "I'm tired," he said when he arrived in Stockholm. "All the publicity . . . the clowning . . . the headlines, the pressure, my domestic problems. It all took a lot out of me. You can't go strong all the time, and my old stunts don't work no more."[8]

> "This is a hard way to make a living. I'm getting old."[7]

In 1966, he defended his title twice in London, England, first on May 21 and then August 6. The May fight was against Henry Cooper and after six rounds, Ali was declared not only the winner, but possibly the best

Jogging alongside the queen's royal horses on their morning run helped Ali train for his title fight against British champ Henry Cooper.

heavyweight in boxing history, according to British sports-writers. In August, he faced Brian London at the same location. After three rounds, London fell unconscious.

Ali moved on to Frankfurt, Germany, next, where he fought Karl Mildenberger. It was a difficult match and lasted twelve rounds before Ali won, retaining his title.

Returning to the United States, Ali fought a match against Cleveland Williams in the Astrodome in Houston, Texas. Williams was a powerful fighter who hoped to destroy Ali. But the November 16, 1966, fight saw Ali dancing around Williams, throwing quick, stiff jabs. Williams fell after three rounds.

In 1967, Ali had two more fights. He finally settled his title dispute with Ernie Terrell on February 6 in New York. Although it took a full fifteen rounds and was not a pretty fight, Ali came away with the victory.

Still, some people remained unimpressed. Former heavyweight champion Joe Louis said, "Cassius Clay's got lots of ability, but he is not The Greatest. He's a guy with a million dollars' worth of confidence and a dime's worth of courage. . . . Trouble with Clay, he thinks he knows it all. Fights with his mouth. He won't listen."[9]

Ali's bout on March 22, 1967, was against Zora Folley. Held in New York, the fight went seven rounds. Folley never looked confident, and he missed his punches as Ali danced around him. Folley finally fell from a punch to his jaw. Although Ali had won, it would be his last fight for more than three years.

Ali was scheduled to be inducted into the U.S. Army on April 11, 1967. Attorneys postponed the date until two and a half weeks later. During that time, Ali made it clear how he felt about the situation. "Why should they ask me to put on a uniform and go ten thousand miles from home

Civil rights leader Martin Luther King, Jr.,
supported Ali's objection to fighting in the army.

and drop bombs and bullets on brown people in Vietnam while so-called Negro people in Louisville are treated like dogs?" he asked.[10]

Ali did not intend to join the army. He was willing to be jailed for his refusal to serve in the armed forces. "What's wrong with me going to jail for something I believe in?" Ali asked. "Boys are dying in Vietnam for something they don't believe."[11]

He arrived at the examining and entrance headquarters in Houston at eight in the morning on April 28, 1967. He was one of twenty-six men scheduled to be inducted that day. He filled out forms, took physical examinations, and ate lunch.

> "What's wrong with me going to jail for something I believe in?"

With a few demonstrators standing outside in support of Ali's refusal to be drafted, the induction ceremony began in the early afternoon. As each man's name was called, he was supposed to step forward, indicating that he had now joined the armed forces.

When Ali's name was called—"Cassius Marcellus Clay"—he did not step forward. "I have searched my conscience and I find I cannot be true to my belief by accepting such a call," he said.[12]

Ali was led to another room. Here, he was informed that he might have to serve up to five years in prison and pay a $10,000 fine for his actions. Ali said he knew this but was refusing to be drafted because of his beliefs.

Reporters crowded around Ali after his refusal
to be inducted into the army in April 1967.

"He's fighting for the respect of his religion. He's
not fighting his country," said Drew Brown, his assistant
trainer.[13]

Ali later said that he felt a sense of relief after the
induction ceremony. He did what he believed was
the right thing to do. "If I was in the service I could not be
teaching anything about the Holy Koran," Ali said. "I'd
be going against it. I'd be a hypocrite."[14]

The American public was split as to how it felt about Ali's refusal to join the armed forces and fight in Vietnam. Some people cheered his decision, while many others thought he was betraying his country.

Only one hour after Ali took a stand against his induction, the New York State Athletic Commission suspended his boxing license and took away his title. Other jurisdictions—including the World Boxing Association—quickly did the same. Ali's U.S. passport was also confiscated, so he could not travel outside the United States.

Still, Ali said, "I feel better than when I beat the eight-to-one odds and won the World Heavyweight Title from Liston."[15]

Although he had not been defeated in the ring, Ali had lost his heavyweight crown. He was no longer the champion of the world.

Chapter 9

Regaining the Title

On June 20, 1967, Ali was found guilty of refusing to be inducted into the U.S. armed forces. He was sentenced to five years in prison, but remained free on bail. Ali's lawyers would spend the next four years trying to get the conviction overturned.

Banned from fighting in the ring, Ali turned instead to fighting problems in American society. He protested the unfair treatment of black people. He also spoke out against the war in Vietnam. He said that war, in general, was wrong "unless you have a very good reason to kill."[1]

Some newspaper reporters attacked Ali for taking a stand against the war. But as the years moved on, thousands of Americans began to object to the country's involvement in Vietnam. Many people were put into prison for refusing to fight in the war. Others ran away to

Canada so they would not have to serve in the United States Armed Forces. Many colleges, where the Vietnam War was unpopular with students, welcomed Ali and his antiwar message.

During this time, Ali married Belinda Boyd. She was seventeen years old and had been raised as a Black Muslim. The couple would go on to have four children together: Maryum, Rasheeda and

> Banned from fighting in the ring, Ali turned instead to fighting problems in American society.

Jamillah, who were twins, and Muhammad Jr.

Ali adored his children. He enjoyed indulging them as much as he disliked disciplining them. Often, Ali would buy them presents, even when it was not their birthday or a holiday. If the children wanted a cookie or some kind of treat before dinner, they knew their mother would say no. So they would ask their father, who always gave in.

Ali's money was running low, and he needed to find ways of supporting his family. He was asked to appear in a documentary of his life, and he agreed. Ali was paid $1,000 a day—in cash—for a period of one week. The film was called *A/K/A Cassius Clay* and would eventually do well when it was released a couple of years later.

Ali also appeared in the lead role of a black-themed Broadway musical. Theater critics were generally surprised at the quality of Ali's performance. His singing and

Belinda Boyd and Ali were married at his home on Chicago's South Side on August 19, 1967.

acting were praised in reviews, and the charm of his personality made him a natural onstage. Unfortunately, the show, called *Buck White*, closed after only one week.

Ali was banished from the world of boxing for a total of three and a half years. By 1970, Ali was focused on one thought. He wanted to regain his title as heavyweight champion. But how could Ali fight if he was not even allowed in the ring? Most states have an athletic commission that votes on whether or not to give a boxer a license to fight. More than twenty states refused to give Ali— considered a draft dodger—a license. But Georgia had no athletic commission. The decision rested with the mayor of Atlanta, Sam Massell. When Massell gave his okay, a match was set up for October 26, 1970. Ali's opponent would be Jerry Quarry.

Ali had not fought in a professional bout since the spring of 1967. "They're expecting me to come back looking fat, looking bad," he said. "They think they've done me in. But I'm going to fool them."[2]

In the first round, Ali moved lightly on his feet in his usual style. He landed most of his punches and looked strong. But he began to slow down in the second round, and when Quarry hit him with some tough blows to his body, it seemed as if Quarry might emerge as the winner. Ali was not on his toes in the third round. He stood flat-footed, then he landed a punch that opened a deep gash over Quarry's eye. Between rounds three and four,

**Before his fight against Jerry Quarry in 1970,
Ali joked with reporters at a news conference inside the ring.**

Quarry's cornerman and the referee halted the action, awarding the victory to Ali by technical knockout in round three.

Ali had definitely slowed down since his layoff. Yet he fought again six weeks later. A court order allowed him to fight in New York, and the December bout took place in

Madison Square Garden. He fought Oscar Bonavena, and the match ended in the fifteenth round. Ali delivered a left hook that knocked his opponent down. Bonavena got up but was knocked down two more times. Ali won by a technical knockout.

While Ali was banned from the ring, Joe Frazier was considered the world's heavyweight champion. Joe Frazier had knocked out Jimmy Ellis to take the title. Frazier had grown up on a South Carolina farm with twelve siblings. From the time he was a young boy, Frazier knew what he wanted to be when he grew up. "I had one thing in mind,"

Jerry Quarry

Quarry was a smart boxer with a good left hook. At six feet and 195 pounds, Quarry was smaller and lighter than Ali. He had won the National Golden Gloves championship in 1965, gaining fame for being the only boxer to knock out all of his opponents on his way to capturing that title. Quarry then turned professional and won all fourteen of his fights that first year. When the World Boxing Association had held a tournament to replace Ali, Quarry took part. He made it to the finals, where he lost to Jimmy Ellis. In the later years of his life, Quarry suffered from severe brain damage, caused by repeated blows to the head. He died in 1999.

Ali stands victorious over
Oscar Bonavena, December 7, 1970.

he said, "being the heavyweight champion of the world. And I was a little guy—but a little guy with a big mind and a big body, and big punches."[3]

Frazier won the gold medal in 1964 at the Tokyo Olympic Games in the heavyweight division—even though he was fighting with a broken thumb. Over the course of six years, the soft-spoken fighter had never lost a match. Out of twenty-six fights, he had won twenty-three by knockout.

"Being a fighter made a good living for me," Frazier said later, "but that wasn't all. I loved fighting. I loved the competitiveness. I loved to stand on my own. People don't understand what an honor it is to be a fighter. It gave me the best opportunity to prove myself, to stand up and say, 'I'm the best; I matter; I am.'"[4]

Frazier was eager to fight Ali to prove he deserved the title. He had even made a New Year's resolution concerning Ali. "I was going to dust that butterfly off," he said. "I was going to clip his wings. I was going to slow him down. I wanted to show him who was the greatest."[5]

Ali wanted to fight Frazier to get back the crown he believed was rightfully his. "For Joe Frazier to be the champion, he's got to beat me," said Ali.[6] The fight was held in Madison Square Garden on March 8, 1971. It was the most talked-about fight in the history of boxing, and it also had the largest purse of any fight: Both Ali and

Ali trained hard for his fight against Joe Frazier in 1971.

Frazier would receive two and a half million dollars each. Thirty-five countries would broadcast the match live.

As usual, Ali—who was known for his rhyming boasts—had something to say about fighting Frazier:

> *"I'm gonna come out smokin',*
> *And I won't be jokin'.*
> *I'm gonna be a peckin' and a pokin',*
> *Pouring water on his smokin'.*
> *It might shock you and amaze ya,*
> *But I'm gonna destroy Joe Frazier!"*[7]

Frazier seemed confident of victory and predicted he would win in ten rounds or less. Ali seemed equally sure of winning. "If he's going to hit me in the body, he's got to get within hitting range, and when he gets there, he'll be within MY hitting range," Ali said. "He's easy to jab, easy to hit. And as long as I can land, it's all over."[8]

> For once, Ali was unable to live up to his boasts.

But for once, Ali was unable to live up to his boasts. Although the fight began evenly, Ali's legs were not as quick as they had once been. He was often forced to lean against the ropes and take the blows Frazier was delivering.

After the ninth round, Ali saw that he had also inflicted injuries on Frazier. He was bleeding from his nose and mouth and above his eye. "But he won't go down," said Ali later. "Now I know he'll die before he quits."[9]

By the eleventh round, it was clear that Ali was hurting, and in the final round Ali took a blow to his jaw that threw him to the ground. Somehow he got up and finished the fight, but Frazier won by unanimous decision.

"You put up a great fight," Frazier told him.

Ali replied, "You the Champ."[10]

The fight had been hard for Ali, whose face was even more swollen and misshapen than Frazier's when the fight ended. He described what it was like to be hit by someone with Frazier's power:

> Take a stiff tree branch in your hand and hit it against the floor and you'll feel your hand go *boinggggggg*. Well, getting tagged is the same kind of jaw on your whole body, and you need at least ten or twenty seconds to make that go away. You get hit again before that, you got another *boingggggg*. . . . You can't think. You're just numb and you don't know where you're at. There's no *pain*, just that jarring feeling. But I automatically know what to do when that happens to me, sort of like a sprinkler system going off when a fire starts up.[11]

Ali said his three and a half years in exile had resulted in his being out of shape. Perhaps if he had fought Frazier when he was younger, the fight might have ended differently. But Frazier punched hard, Ali said, and had earned the victory.

After the fight, Ali was taken to the hospital. He was limp, not even able to dress himself. His jaw was X-rayed, and although he was encouraged to stay the night at the hospital so the medical staff could keep an eye on him, Ali refused. He did not want to give anyone the opportunity to say that Joe Frazier had put him in the hospital.

Ali was calm when he faced reporters the following day. "Just lost a fight, that's all," he said. "There are more important things to worry about in life. Probably be a better man for it."[12]

It had now been four years since Ali had refused to serve in the U.S. armed forces. "I don't have to be what you want me to be," Ali maintained. "I'm free to be who I want."[13]

His lawyers had been trying to appeal the criminal charges against him. On June 28, 1971, the U.S. Supreme Court unanimously overturned Ali's conviction for refusing to be inducted. This decision was based on a technicality. To be considered a conscientious objector, Ali had been ordered to show three things: (1) he did not believe in war; (2) this opposition was based on his religious beliefs; (3) his feelings were sincere.

> "I don't have to be what you want me to be."

The draft board, however, had not mentioned specifically which of these conditions Ali had failed to meet. By using this technicality to overturn the ruling against Ali, the Supreme Court was making its decision only in Ali's case. The Justices were not saying that all Black Muslims could be considered conscientious objectors.

Interestingly, Ali's experiences of the previous three years seemed to endear him to many Americans, and his popularity increased. "He lost three years of his ability as a boxer," said Juan Williams, senior correspondent with National Public Radio. "But once he had paid the price, even people who disagreed with Ali, even people who thought, 'This is a big blabbermouth. This guy's a lot of hot air,' said 'You know what? He paid the price.' And any time an American pays the price, other Americans say, 'That's my man.'"[14]

Ali had been allowed back in the ring, and his passport was returned to him. But if he wanted to get the title of heavyweight champion back, Ali would have to do that himself.

Chapter 10

The Hardest Battle

li's goal was to fight a rematch with Frazier and once again become the champion. On the road to that fight, he faced a dozen opponents.

In July 1971, Ali faced Jimmy Ellis. The two had been friends and sparring partners years earlier back in Louisville. Ellis knew all Ali's moves and felt confident about beating him. He knew Ali's legs were not what they had once been and that he had slowed down. Still, in the twelfth round, Ali knocked out Ellis and won the match.

After Ellis, Ali took on Buster Mathis and won with little difficulty. In fact, Ali was criticized by the press for going easy on Mathis and not hitting him as hard as he could have. But Ali stated that he had no interest in killing the man. He just wanted to win the fight. "How do I know just how hard to hit him to knock him out and not hurt

**Cassius Clay Sr., center, with his two sons,
Muhammad Ali, left, and Rahaman Ali (formerly Rudy Clay).**

him?" Ali asked. "I don't care about looking good to the fans, I got to look good to God."[1]

At the end of the year, Ali traveled to Switzerland to fight Jurgen Blin of West Germany. He knocked out Blin in seven rounds. In April 1972, Ali fought Mac Foster in Tokyo, Japan, and won in fifteen rounds. He then moved on to Vancouver, British Columbia, to take on George Chuvalo, his opponent of six years earlier. He won by decision in his May 1972 match against Chuvalo. In June, he fought Jerry Quarry again, winning the fight by a technical knockout in seven rounds. Ali won another technical knockout against Al "Blue" Lewis in a match held in Dublin, Ireland, later that summer.

Ali now took off two months before his next fight. He was asked to star in a movie called *Heaven Can Wait*. He was to receive $250,000 for his work, and he was looking forward to it. But Elijah Muhammad, leader of the Nation of Islam, did not like the project. The plot of the film revolved around the untimely death of an athlete who is allowed to return to earth in the body of another man. Muhammad said this went against Muslim beliefs because the religious group did not believe in life after death. Ali did not make the movie.

In early fall 1972, Ali decided to undertake a project that had interested him for a long time. He opened a training center in Deer Lake, Pennsylvania. The $42,000

Deer Lake Training Center

Ali's training center was run differently from facilities where other celebrated boxers trained. Several other boxers did not allow anyone around when they were training. But Ali wanted Deer Lake to be open to everyone. When he saw that his wife, Belinda, had put up a rope outside the facility, he asked her to take it down. He wanted people to know they were welcome.

facility included a large gym, a dining hall, a barn, a bungalow, and guest cabins. Remembering the large boulders standing near Archie Moore's training center, Ali painted the names of former champions on the rocks outside his center. Ali trained at Deer Lake for the next nine years.

Ali took advantage of his fame and used it to help others. He frequently visited hospitals and spent time with children who were very ill or crippled. He hugged them

Ali always worked out vigorously to stay in shape.

and kissed them, and the children loved him. Ali did the same at nursing homes, visiting many elderly patients who were bedridden. He would talk to them for hours. Ali enjoyed people and took pleasure in making them happy.

In September 1972, Ali fought a rematch with Floyd Patterson at Madison Square Garden. Ali won by technical knockout in seven rounds. Two months later, Ali knocked out Bob Foster—the light-heavyweight champion—in Nevada in eight rounds.

The first fight of 1973 for Ali saw him in the ring with Joe Bugner. Ali won a decision after twelve rounds. His next opponent was Ken Norton, and Ali was extremely confident about the match. He did little training—not even three weeks—and less worrying. Norton was twenty-seven years old and had turned pro six years earlier. He was not a graceful boxer, but he had a lot of power and was in excellent shape. Norton had attended college for two years on a football scholarship. Then he left college to join the Marines. There, he began his boxing career.

> Ali enjoyed people and took pleasure in making them happy.

The fight was held in March in San Diego, California. Norton was in good shape, and for several months he had been sparring with Joe Frazier. In the second round, Ali leaned back to avoid a punch from Norton. Then Norton threw a follow-up punch that broke Ali's jaw. Although he was in terrible pain, Ali did not want the fight stopped. He concentrated on protecting his jaw.

As the fight entered the final round, the three judges differed as to who was winning. One judge said the men had the same number of points. Another put Norton ahead by one point, and the third judge had Ali the leader by two points.

Ali managed to finish the bout, but Norton won by split decision. "That night I could have beaten Godzilla," said Norton. "I was that sure of myself. And in that kind of shape, I could have fought for fifty rounds, easy. I was just so cocky at that point. I knew before the bell rang, in my head and in my camp, that I was going to win the fight."[2]

Ali went to the hospital after the fight, and surgeons worked on repairing his jaw for more than nine hours.

Ali wanted to fight Norton again and win. Many doubted he could do it—and some said he would never again become world heavyweight champion. But Ali was determined. It took six months for his jaw to heal, and Ali trained hard. This time, he would not enter the ring over-confident.

The rematch was held on September 10 in Los Angeles, California. This match, too, went twelve rounds, too. Again, no man was the obvious winner as the fight went into its twelfth and final round. The decision was close, but Ali prevailed in the last three minutes and won by unanimous decision.

"The only difference was that for the first fight I weighed about 210," said Norton. "I thought if I went down in weight, I'd be quicker. I went down to about 201 pounds. And I was weaker. The last part of the fight, I tired out."[3]

After winning a decision against Rudy Lubbers the following month in Indonesia, Ali was ready for a rematch with Frazier.

The fight was set for January 28, 1974, and tensions between the two boxers were mounting. Only a few days earlier, Ali and Frazier had appeared on television on *ABC Sports* to promote the bout and had gotten into a physical fight after exchanging insults. The New York State Athletic Commission fined each man $5,000 for misconduct in the TV studio.

As usual, Ali appeared confident. "I'm not predicting the round, but I'm predicting I'll do what I should've done the first time," he said. "No layin' on the ropes. I'll be dancin', stickin', in and out, I'll be moving. Moving fast. This will be an amateur meeting a great professional. No contest."[4]

The fight was not a repeat of their matchup three years earlier. Ali did not spend as much time resting against the ropes. Instead, he dealt numerous jabs to Frazier's forehead. Frazier concentrated more on hitting Ali's body

Ali was mobbed by fans outside a
movie theater playing a film about his life.

than his head, yet in the final rounds he was obviously tired. Ali won the match by decision. He said he won because of his rigorous training regimen at his camp in Pennsylvania. "If it wasn't for Deer Lake, I woulda lost. I had a little more stamina this time, didn't I?" he asked.[5]

When Ali was asked how he managed to deal with Frazier's punches, he said, "Because I'm skillful enough to get out of trouble."[6]

Eager to win back his heavyweight title, Ali had to take on George Foreman, who wore the world crown at this time. Foreman was in his mid-twenties and known for his incredibly hard punches. He had been a bully as a boy and had frequently gotten into trouble. When he developed an interest in boxing, Foreman realized from the start that he had talent. In 1968, he won the gold medal at the Mexico City Olympic Games.

Foreman began fighting professionally the next year and won eleven fights by knockout. In 1973, he took the ring against Joe Frazier. Foreman knocked out Frazier in the second round and claimed the world heavyweight title.

Facing Ali in 1974, Foreman said, "If he thinks this is going to be all work and no education, he's mistaken."[7] Foreman had first met Ali six years earlier, during the time that Ali was banned from boxing. Foreman had been training in Florida when Ali walked into the gym one day and told Foreman he had something to show him. Ali soon returned with a briefcase.

"I thought, this guy's going to show me maybe a hundred thousand dollars in cash," Foreman said. "And he opened the briefcase and there was a telephone in it. 'See, it's a briefcase telephone,' he [Ali] said. It wasn't working. It wasn't hooked up. But the point of it is, he was like a kid."[8]

The fight was called the "Rumble in the Jungle" and was held in Kinshasa, Zaire. Almost no one thought Ali could win. He was thirty-two years old and past his prime as a fighter. Foreman had not yet lost a fight, and thirty-seven of his forty wins had been knockouts. In addition to this, not only had Foreman beaten Joe Frazier, but he had also defeated Ken Norton—the boxer who had recently beaten Ali in a two-round match.

Ali and Foreman each received $5 million from the president of Zaire for the "Rumble in the Jungle." Never before had a boxer earned this much for a fight. In fact, it was more than the boxing stars Joe Louis and Jack Dempsey had earned in their entire careers.

The fight was originally slated for September 25, 1974. But Foreman received a bad cut to his eye while sparring a week before the match. The fight was postponed until October 30, 1974, when sixty thousand fans showed up for the fight.

As usual, Ali kept up a patter of talk—even right before the fight when the referee was giving the two boxers their instructions.

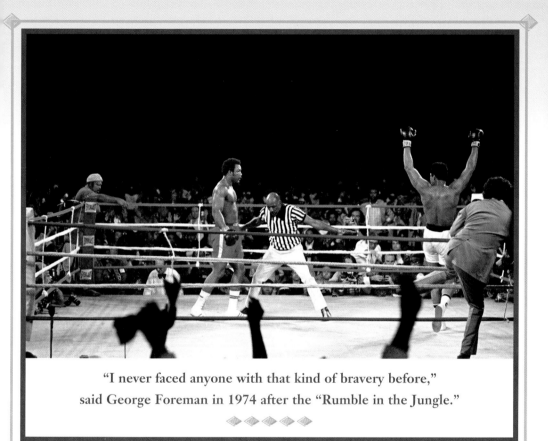

"I never faced anyone with that kind of bravery before,"
said George Foreman in 1974 after the "Rumble in the Jungle."

"Never mind that stuff, sucker," Ali said. "I'm gonna hit you everywhere but under the bottom of your big funky feet, chump! You got to go, sucker."

The referee told him, "Ali, I warned you. Be quiet!"[9] Ali continued taunting Foreman until the referee threatened to disqualify him.

Ali's original plan for this match was "to dance every round. I had it in mind to do what I did when I was twenty-two but I got tired, so I had to change my strategy."[10]

Ali's change of strategy was unusual. Since Foreman was known for his hard punches, Ali let him punch. He leaned back against the ropes and protected himself from the blows with his forearms and elbows—fighting off the ropes rather than moving around the ring.

> Ali kept up the usual boastful comments that infuriated most of his opponents.

"It was a huge, brilliant gamble," said boxing writer Mark Kram, "and one that could have backfired on him very easily. I mean, it was staying on the ropes being hit."[11]

Through it all, Ali kept up the usual boastful comments that infuriated most of his opponents. "I must not let him think his blows can stop me from talking," he remembered thinking. "If I stop talking now, he knows I'm hurt."[12]

So Ali continued. "Come on, George, show me something," he said. "Can't you fight harder? That ain't hard. I thought you was the Champion, I thought you had punches."[13]

Not only did Foreman tire, but he began to question his punching ability. After all, Ali was just *taking* the punches.

As Foreman slugged away, he said Ali tauntingly asked him, "'That all you got, George?' And I remember thinking, 'Yup. That's about it.'"[14]

Although no trainer ever would have advised a boxer

to fight off the ropes—a technique later called rope-a-dope—Ali's strategy worked. Foreman was exhausted, and soon Ali began landing his own punches on the wearying fighter. In the eighth round, Ali knocked him out and won the match.

"I lost," said Foreman. "He beat me fair and square. The guy could fight. He could punch."[15]

Before the fight, Ali had said he would retire no matter what the outcome. But his feelings seemed to change after the victory. "They took my title away from me unjustly and I want to hang on to it for a few months," he said.[16]

Foreman had only praise for Ali, although this was the first time he had been knocked out since turning professional. "A true champion never complains, never bad-mouths an opponent," he said. "I think Ali should be respected. He's a true American, a great gentleman and he should be called the champion."[17]

Ali reaped the rewards of his victory almost instantly. *Sports Illustrated* magazine named him Sportsman of the Year and President Gerald Ford invited him to the White House.

Ali fought and won three matches in 1975—against Chuck Wepner, Ron Lyle, and Joe Bugner—before facing Frazier for the third time. Billed as the "Thrilla in Manila," the fight took place on October 1 in Quezon, Philippines.

"Manila wasn't about the heavyweight championship of the world. There was something much more important at stake," said Thomas Hauser, an expert on boxing and Ali. "Muhammad Ali and Joe Frazier were fighting for the heavyweight championship of each other. They both understood that whoever won this fight, well, that's who history was going to recognize as the greater fighter."[18]

Publicity for the fight was huge, because each held a victory from his two previous encounters. In addition, they seemed to honestly dislike each other. "He not only looks bad! You can smell him in another country!" shouted Ali. "Ignorant. Stupid. Ugly. If he's champ again, other nations will laugh at us."[19]

Ali predicted an easy victory for himself. "This fight won't even be close," said Ali after going through his final workout. "Not one round will the judges say Joe Frazier won. . . . Joe Frazier is completely washed up, nothin' but a punchin' bag."[20]

Frazier's response was that the fight could last the full fifteen rounds. "Anywhere from one to fifteen, I'll be there," he said. "I ain't goin' nowhere."[21]

From the start of the fight, Ali came out intentionally flat-footed. He did not dance that night; he hit. Frazier hit, too. "Joe Frazier, they told me you were washed up," Ali said, as he and Frazier moved around the ring.

Frazier responded, "They told you wrong, pretty boy."[22]

In the sixth round, Frazier smashed two hooks to Ali's jaw. Although Ali's legs buckled, he took the punches. After ten rounds, the two men were exhausted and badly beaten up. Ali told Dundee, "This is the closest that I've ever been to dying."[23]

The fight continued, and Frazier hit hard at Ali's face. Ali called on whatever strength he had left to retaliate. Frazier's mouthpiece was bloody as it went flying out of his mouth, and his eyes were practically swollen shut from the blows he had suffered. He could barely see.

Yet when Frazier's cornerman told the referee to stop the fight, Frazier yelled, "No, no, no! You can't do that to me!"

"Sit down, son," said trainer Eddie Futch. "It's over. No one will forget what you did here today."[24]

The fight had come to an end. Ali had won in fourteen rounds. Many boxing experts consider it the greatest fight in history.

"He could have whupped anybody in the world except me," Ali said of Frazier. "He is great. He is greater than I thought he was. He is the best there is except me."[25]

Although Frazier intensely disliked Ali, he had to admire him. "Man, I hit him with punches that bring down the walls of a city. What held him up?"[26]

Ali was now approaching his mid-thirties. Although he was showing tremendous courage in the ring, it was questionable how much more physical punishment his body could take. He talked about quitting, and many people who were close to him urged him to retire from boxing. Yet Ali continued to fight for five more years. In 1976, he won four bouts including a fifteen-round victory over Ken Norton. He won both of his fights in 1977, against Alfredo Evangelista and Ernie Shavers.

At this time, Ali's marriage to Belinda Ali ended. He had met another woman, Veronica Porche. Porche had been chosen as a poster girl to promote the Ali-Foreman fight. They began spending time together and had a child, Hana. Ali and Porche married on June 19, 1977.

The year 1978 saw Ali lose his title in fifteen rounds to Leon Spinks, an average fighter whom Ali could have easily beaten when he was younger. Seven months after losing to Spinks, Ali fought him again and this time came out on top after fifteen rounds. In winning this fight, Ali captured the title for a third time.

Although Ali announced his retirement in 1979, he returned to boxing the following year and lost by technical knockout to Larry Holmes in round eleven. Ali was barely able to put up a fight, and Holmes pleaded with the referee to stop the match. "I'm going to hurt him," he told the ref.[27]

Finally, Ali fought and lost a ten-round decision—his last fight—on December 1981, to Trevor Berbick.

Ali ended his career with a final record of fifty-six wins and five losses. Thirty-seven of his wins were knockouts.

He was the first boxer to win the world heavyweight title three times. While his record is not the best in the history of boxing, Ali made a place for himself through his fighting, his courage, and the sheer strength of his personality.

Veronica and Muhammad Ali

Ali's health deteriorated as the years went on. In 1984 Ali's doctors diagnosed the boxer with Parkinson's syndrome, a collection of symptoms that mimic Parkinson's disease. There is no known cause for Parkinson's syndrome, although head injuries have been linked to it. The illness makes it difficult for Ali to walk and talk. His limbs shake, and his facial expression often seems frozen. In spite of this, doctors said he could expect to have a normal life span.

Ali views the illness from a religious point of view.

> God tries you in certain, certain ways. Some people are rich and they believe in God. They lose the money, things get hard, they get weak and quit going to church. . . . I won the title, became champion. Powerful and strong. Good looking. And then God

tries you, take my health. Fixes it so it's hard to talk. Hard to walk. To see if you're still pretty, see if you still worship. . . . This is a trial from God.[28]

Meanwhile, Ali's marriage to Veronica Ali was coming to an end. They had had three more children together—Miya, Khalilah, and Laila, but the couple finally decided the marriage was not working. They divorced in the summer of 1986.

That same year, Ali married Yolanda "Lonnie" Williams. She had known Ali since she was in first grade. He was fourteen years older than Lonnie and had lived

Ali and Lonnie Williams were married in Louisville, Kentucky.

across the street from her family in Louisville, Kentucky. By the time Lonnie was seventeen, she had a crush on Ali. They remained friends through the years, and on November 20, 1986, they married. Lonnie had been raised as a Catholic but had begun studying the beliefs of Islam. They had one child, Asaad Amin, whom they adopted.

In the summer of 1996, Ali was chosen to

light the Olympic flame in Atlanta, Georgia, and begin the Olympic Summer Games there. Many of the 3.5 billion people who watched the event on television were moved to tears as they saw the three-time heavyweight champion slowly make his way up the stadium steps, his hand visibly shaking from his illness as he held the Olympic torch.

Lonnie Ali said that her husband also seemed deeply affected by the event. He remained sitting a long while in a chair in his hotel room holding on to the torch, which was no longer aflame. The positive response he received from the public seemed to give him courage, she said, showing him "that people won't slight his message because of his impairment."[29] She said his message is "love." Even well into the 1990s, Ali focused on spreading that love to others and devoting himself to helping other people. To earn money, he visited conventions and industrial shows around the world, charging up to $200,000 for an appearance. He also attended charity events for organizations such as UNICEF, Sisters of the Poor, and Best Buddies, which helps the mentally impaired. He has given of his time generously and has never hesitated to approach someone with a serious or infectious illness. He hugs children and shakes everyone's hand. When a Roman Catholic nun wrote to Ali, asking for his help with the Liberian children she was caring for

Ali carried the torch during the opening ceremonies
of the Olympic Summer Games in 1996.

at a mission, he showed up the following month to give out food himself.

Lunchtime has often found Ali at the local McDonald's, in his special corner, where he has always enjoyed talking to children in the neighborhood. The youths in the area have often spoken to Ali through the intercom at the main gate of his estate, inviting the former boxing champ to come out and play. At home on his eighty-one-acre farm in Berrien Springs, Michigan, Ali has signed countless pictures of himself and put his name on brochures to be distributed about the Islamic religion. Five times a day, he faces Mecca to say prayers.

Ali is also an author. His autobiography, *The Greatest: My Own Story*, came out in 1975, written with Richard Durham. Ali's 2004 book, *The Soul of a Butterfly: Reflections on Life's Journey*, was written with his daughter Hana Yasmeen Ali. In this work, Ali discusses very little of his life as a boxer. Instead, the book is a collection of spiritual thoughts that have inspired him through the years, touching on such topics as God, love, and the responsibilities that go along with being a celebrity.

Ali's daughter Laila has followed her father's footsteps, becoming a successful boxer since her debut in 1999. She received a lot of attention in 2001, when she fought and defeated Jacqui Frazier, daughter of the former heavyweight champion Joe Frazier.

Ali has always loved children—and they, in turn, adore him.

Parkinson's did not cause Ali to retreat from life in the public eye. The illness, however, has increasingly taken its toll on the former heavyweight champion. In recent years, he has slowed down considerably and is unable to participate in as many activities. Still, Ali has never wanted anyone to feel sorry for him. "I'm the same person, a little more settled," he has said. "A little more cool and calm. Not as fast as I was. That's about all."[30]

A museum honoring the boxer scheduled its opening gala events for November 2005. The Muhammad Ali Center in Louisville, Kentucky, houses twenty-four thousand square feet of displays and exhibits that tell the story of Ali's life. The goal is to encourage children and adults to work their hardest and do their best. The six-story building includes a library and classroom space for educational programs. The cost of creating the center topped $40 million, and officials hope the museum will attract 350,000 visitors each year.

Ali says he does not miss boxing nor would he change anything about his life. "Everything has a purpose," he said. "I wouldn't change nothin'. It all turned out good."[31]

"Most people in this country get a little sickness, especially if they've been . . . celebrities, and they hide," said George Foreman after the 1996 Olympics. "They won't come out. Someone has something like Parkinson's, they'll just stay in the house and hide. . . . This guy came up with that torch shaking and lighting that thing like that—I felt so proud of him. Muhammad Ali did a lot for the world when he did that . . . to see him do it and not be ashamed. To say, 'I am the greatest and still alive.'"[32]

Even into the twenty-first century, the name Muhammad Ali has not lost its impact. When he was a young man, Ali declared that he would be the greatest in

Ali in February 2005 at a tribute in his honor.

the world. In many ways, he became bigger than even he expected. Ali's fame went beyond boxing and beyond sports. For many years, his was the most recognized face in the world.

As for how Ali would like people to think of him, he has said, "I'll tell you how I'd like to be remembered: as a black man who won the heavyweight title and who was humorous and who treated everyone right. As a man who never looked down on those who looked up to him and who helped as many of his people as he could. . . . If that's asking too much, then I guess I'd settle for being remembered only as a great boxer who became a preacher and a champion of his people. And I wouldn't even mind if folks forgot how pretty I was."[33]

Chronology

1942—Cassius Clay Jr. is born in Louisville, Kentucky, to Odessa and Cassius Sr.

1954—Begins boxing with police officer and part-time boxing trainer Joe Martin.

1957—Begins attending Central High School.

1960—Wins the gold medal in the light-heavyweight division at the Rome Olympics. Becomes a professional boxer.

1964—Defeats heavyweight champion Sonny Liston and wins world heavyweight title. Joins the Nation of Islam and changes his name to Muhammad Ali.

1965—Defeats Liston a second time.

1966—Defends title in U.S. and Europe.

1967—Refuses to be drafted into the armed forces; is stripped of his heavyweight title and banned from the boxing ring.

1969—Appears on Broadway in the title role of the musical *Buck White*.

1970—Wins comeback fight against Jerry Quarry.

1971—Fights heavyweight champion Joe Frazier and loses by unanimous decision. Supreme Court reverses his conviction for refusing induction into the army.

1972—Opens his boxing training center in Deer Lake, Pennsylvania.

CHRONOLOGY

1973—Loses to Ken Norton by unanimous decision, then wins rematch against Norton.

1974—Beats Joe Frazier in twelve rounds. Knocks out George Foreman in "Rumble in the Jungle" to regain heavyweight championship title. Named "Sportsman of the Year" by *Sports Illustrated* magazine.

1975—Wins his third fight against Frazier, called the "Thrilla in Manila." Ali's autobiography, *The Greatest*, written with Richard Durham, is published by Random House, Inc.

1978—Loses the heavyweight title to Leon Spinks, then wins it back, becoming the first three-time heavyweight champion of the world.

1979—Announces his retirement from boxing.

1980—Comes out of retirement; loses to Larry Holmes.

1981—Loses the final fight of his career to Trevor Berbick. Retires with overall professional record of 56–5.

1984—Diagnosed with Parkinson's syndrome.

1988—Receives a lifetime achievement award from the United Nations.

1996—Carries the Olympic Torch at the opening ceremonies of the Summer Olympics in Atlanta, Georgia.

1999—His daughter Laila debuts as a boxer.

2005—Muhammad Ali Center opens.

Chapter Notes

Chapter 1. Learning the Ropes

1. John Miller and Aaron Kenedi, eds., *Muhammad Ali: Ringside* (Boston: Little, Brown and Company, 1999), p. 18.

2. David Remnick, *King of the World: Muhammad Ali and the Rise of the American Hero* (New York: Random House, 1998), p. 91.

3. Ibid., p. 92.

4. Muhammad Ali with Richard Durham, *The Greatest: My Own Story* (New York: Random House, 1975), p. 46.

5. Ibid.

6. Ibid.

7. Remnick, p. 92.

Chapter 2. Somebody Special

1. Robert Lipsyte, "'I Don't Have to Be What You Want Me to Be,' Says Muhammad Ali," *New York Times*, March 7, 1971, p. SM 25.

2. Thomas Hauser, *Muhammad Ali: His Life and Times* (New York: Simon & Schuster, 1991), p. 16.

3. Ibid.

4. José Torres, *Sting Like a Bee: The Muhammad Ali Story* (London: Abelard-Schuman, 1971), p. 84.

5. Ibid.

Chapter 3. In Training

1. José Torres, *Sting Like a Bee: The Muhammad Ali Story* (London: Abelard-Schuman, 1971), pp. 85–86.

2. David Remnick, *King of the World: Muhammad Ali and the Rise of the American Hero* (New York: Random House, 1998), p. 93.

3. Robert Lipsyte, " 'I Don't Have to Be What You Want Me to Be,' Says Muhammad Ali," *New York Times*, March 7, 1971, p. SM24.

4. Thomas Hauser, *Muhammad Ali: His Life and Times* (New York: Simon & Schuster, 1991), p. 19.

CHAPTER NOTES

5. Remnick, p. 94.

6. Hunt Helm, "Louisville Remembers the Shy Kid from Central High," *The Courier-Journal* (Louisville, Kentucky), September 14, 1997.

7. Remnick, p. 95.

8. Muhammad Ali with Richard Durham, *The Greatest: My Own Story* (New York: Random House, 1975), p. 51.

9. Ali, p. 51.

10. Remnick, p. 96.

11. Remnick, p. 98.

12. Thomas Hauser, *Muhammad Ali: His Life and Times* (New York: Simon & Schuster, 1991), p. 35.

13. Remnick, p. 95.

Chapter 4. Going for the Gold

1. David Remnick, *King of the World: Muhammad Ali and the Rise of the American Hero* (New York: Random House, 1998), p. 101.

2. Ibid., p. 102.

3. José Torres, *Sting Like a Bee: The Muhammad Ali Story* (London: Abelard-Schuman, 1971), p. 93.

4. Thomas Hauser, *Muhammad Ali: His Life and Times* (New York: Simon & Schuster, 1991), p. 26.

5. Muhammad Ali with Richard Durham, *The Greatest: My Own Story* (New York: Random House, 1975), p. 52.

6. Remnick, p. 105.

7. Stephen Brunt, *Facing Ali: The Opposition Weighs In* (Guilford, Conn.: Lyons Press, 2002), p. 15.

8. Hauser, p. 31.

9. Ibid., p. 34.

10. Remnick, pp. 112–113.

Chapter 5. Training and Fighting

1. Thomas Hauser, *Muhammad Ali: His Life and Times* (New York: Simon & Schuster, 1991), p. 36.

2. David Remnick, *King of the World: Muhammad Ali and the Rise of the American Hero* (New York: Random House, 1998), p. 117.

3. Hauser, p. 37.

4. Remnick, p. 120.

5. Ibid., p. 121.
6. Hauser, p. 42.
7. Ibid., p. 54.
8. Ibid., p. 55.

Chapter 6. The Greatest

1. *Muhammad Ali, Sports Century* Classic, cable-television documentary, 2000.

2. John Miller & Aaron Kenedi, eds., *Muhammad Ali: Ringside* (Boston: Little, Brown, & Co., 1999), p. 22.

3. Muhammad Ali with Richard Durham, *The Greatest: My Own Story* (New York: Random House, 1975), p. 113.

4. Thomas Hauser, *Muhammad Ali: His Life and Times* (New York: Simon & Schuster, 1991), p. 60.

5. Nick Tosches, *The Devil and Sonny Liston* (New York: Little, Brown and Company, 2000), p. 202.

6. Ali, p. 115.

7. ESPN documentary.

8. Ali, p. 115.

9. Ali, p. 116.

10. Hauser, p. 74.

11. Remnick, p. 192.

12. ESPN documentary.

13. Remnick, p. 195.

14. Miller, pp. 33, 38.

15. Ali, p. 119.

16. Miller, p. 38.

17. Remnick, p. 199.

18. José Torres, *Sting Like a Bee: The Muhammad Ali Story* (London: Abelard-Schuman, 1971), p. 130.

Chapter 7. A New Direction

1. Hana Ali, *More Than a Hero: Muhammad Ali's Life Lessons Presented Through His Daughter's Eyes* (New York: Simon & Schuster, Inc., 2000), p. 26.

2. William Strathmore, *Muhammad Ali: The Unseen Archives* (United Kingdom: Parragon Publishing, 2001), p. 62.

3. Thomas Hauser, *Muhammad Ali: His Life and Times* (New York: Simon & Schuster, 1991), p. 82.

4. Ibid., p. 128.

5. "Army Is Likely to Recheck Clay," *New York Times*, January 5, 1966.

Chapter 8. Another Kind of Fight

1. Howard Bingham and Max Wallace, *Muhammad Ali's Greatest Fight: Cassius Clay vs. the United States of America* (New York: M. Evans and Company, Inc., 2000), p. 97.

2. "Army Is Likely to Recheck Clay," *New York Times*, January 5, 1966, p. 36.

3. Thomas Hauser, *Muhammad Ali: His Life and Times* (New York: Simon & Schuster, 1991), p. 154.

4. Tom Whitaker, "Editor's Note, Columns: Fondarella!" *Philadelphia Weekly*, February 18, 2004, <http://www.philadelphiaweekly.com/view.php?id=6845> (April 16, 2005).

5. José Torres, *Sting Like a Bee: The Muhammad Ali Story* (London: Abelard-Schuman, 1971), p. 152.

6. Stephen Brunt, *Facing Ali: The Opposition Weighs In* (Guilford, Conn.: Lyons Press, 2002), p. 57.

7. William Strathmore, *Muhammad Ali: The Unseen Archives* (United Kingdom: Paragon Publishing, 2001), p. 157.

8. Robert Lipsyte, "The New Cassius: Quiet, Weary," *New York Times*, August 7, 1966.

9. Stanley Weston, ed., *The Best of The Ring: The Bible of Boxing* (Chicago: Bonus Books, Inc., 1996), p. 203.

10. Thomas Hauser, *Muhammad Ali: His Life and Times* (New York: Simon & Schuster, 1991), p. 167.

11. Gerald Early, ed., *The Muhammad Ali Reader* (Hopewell, N.J.: Ecco Press, 1998), p. 83.

12. Robert Lipsyte, "Induction Oath Refused by Clay," *New York Times*, April 29, 1967, p. 1.

13. AP and UPI dispatches, "Clay Refuses Draft, Risks Prison, Loss of Title," *Courier-Journal* (Louisville, Kentucky), April 28, 1967, <http://www.courier-journal.com/ali/timeline/670428_refusedraft.html> (February 23, 2004).

14. Ibid.

15. Muhammad Ali with Richard Durham, *The Greatest: My Own Story* (New York: Random House, 1975), pp. 175–176.

Chapter 9. Regaining the Title

1. "Morning Edition: Interview with Muhammad Ali," Public Broadcasting Service *African American World*, © 2002 Encyclopedia Britannica, <http://www.pbs.org/wnet/aaworld/reference/articles/muhammad_ali.html> (August 1, 2003).

2. Gerald Early, ed., *The Muhammad Ali Reader* (Hopewell, N.J.: Ecco Press, 1998), p. 79.

3. Stephen Brunt, *Facing Ali: The Opposition Weighs In* (Guilford, Conn.: Lyons Press, 2002), p. 107.

4. Thomas Hauser, *The Black Lights: Inside the World of Professional Boxing* (New York : McGraw-Hill, 1986), p. 17.

5. Brunt, p. 117.

6. *Muhammad Ali, ESPN Sports Century* Classic, cable-television documentary, 2000.

7. Muhammad Ali with Richard Durham, *The Greatest: My Own Story* (New York: Random House, 1975), p. 351.

8. Dave Anderson, "Ali Flits Like a Butterfly, Flees Like a Bee," *New York Times*, March 4, 1971, p. 43.

9. Ali, p. 354.

10. Ibid., p. 357.

11. Early, pp. 135–136.

12. Thomas Hauser, *Muhammad Ali: His Life and Times* (New York: Simon & Schuster, 1991), p. 233.

13. Robert Lipsyte, "'I Don't Have to Be What You Want Me to Be,' Says Muhammad Ali," *The New York Times*, March 7, 1971, p. SM24.

14. ESPN documentary.

Chapter 10. The Hardest Battle

1. Thomas Hauser, *Muhammad Ali: His Life and Times* (New York: Simon & Schuster, 1991), p. 242.

2. Stephen Brunt, *Facing Ali: The Opposition Weighs In* (Guilford, Conn.: Lyons Press, 2002), p. 175.

3. Ibid., p. 177.

4. Dave Anderson, "Playful Ali Is 212; Frazier 209, Quiet," *New York Times*, January 28, 1974, p. 21.

5. Steve Cady, "Ali Says 'No Bad Feeling Between Us,' and Talks of Super Fight III," *New York Times*, January 29, 1974, p. 24.

CHAPTER NOTES

6. Ibid.

7. Muhammad Ali with Richard Durham, *The Greatest: My Own Story* (New York: Random House, 1975), p. 405.

8. Brunt, p. 191.

9. Ali, p. 403.

10. Gerald Early, ed., *The Muhammad Ali Reader* (Hopewell, N.J.: Ecco Press, 1998), p. 136.

11. *Muhammad Ali, ESPN Sports Century* Classic, cable-television documentary, 2000.

12. Ali, p. 407.

13. John Miller and Aaron Kenedi, eds., *Muhammad Ali: Ringside* (Boston: Little, Brown and Company, 1999), p. 72.

14. ESPN documentary.

15. Brunt, 197.

16. "Champion Vague on Retiring," *New York Times*, October 30, 1974, p. 52.

17. Ibid.

18. ESPN documentary.

19. Mark Kram, *Ghosts of Manila: The Fateful Blood Feud Between Muhammad Ali and Joe Frazier* (New York: HarperCollins Publishers, 2001), p. 169.

20. Dave Anderson, "Ali Is 2–1 to Win Showdown III," *New York Times*, September 30, 1975, p. 45.

21. Ibid.

22. ESPN documentary.

23. Brunt, p. 122.

24. Kram, p. 187.

25. A Chastened, Sore Ali Praises His Rival," *New York Times*, October 1, 1975.

26. Kram, p. 188.

27. ESPN documentary.

28. Juan Williams, Interview with Muhammad Ali, National Public Radio, <http://www.npr.org/ramfiles/me/20011219.me.mali.extended.ram> (August 10, 2003).

29. William Plummer, "The World's Champion," Up Front section, *People*, January 13, 1997.

30. Juan Williams, National Public Radio interview.

31. Miller and Kenedi, pp. 109–110.

32. Brunt, p. 206.

33. Miller and Kenedi, p. 115.

Further Reading

Buckley, James Jr. *Muhammad Ali*. Milwaukee, Wisc.: World Almanac Library, 2004.

Randy Gordon, *Muhammad Ali*. New York: Grosset & Dunlap, 2001.

Walter Dean Myers, *The Greatest: Muhammad Ali*. New York: Scholastic Press, 2001.

Internet Addresses

Muhammad Ali: The Greatest of All Time. Ali's official Web site
<http://www.ali.com>

Muhammad Ali: The Making of a Champ
<http://www.courier-journal.com/ali>

International Boxing Hall of Fame: Muhammad Ali
<http://www.ibhof.com/ali.htm>

Index

Page numbers for photographs are in **boldface** type.